The Governance of Privacy

T0341635

The Governance of Privacy

Privacy as Process:
The Need for Resilient Governance

Hans de Bruijn

Amsterdam University Press

Cover design: Gijs Mathijs Ontwerpers, Amsterdam
Lay-out: Crius Group, Hulshout

ISBN   978 94 6372 967 3
e-ISBN   978 90 4855 612 0
NUR   740 | 980

© H. de Bruijn / Amsterdam University Press B.V., Amsterdam 2022

Printed and bound by CPI Group (UK) Ltd, Croydon, CR0 4YY

Table of Contents

1   The Radical Transformation of Privacy

1.1   Introduction

Let me start this book with a confession: I have had my doubts concerning the title *The Governance of Privacy*. Why?

In our data-driven world privacy is, on the one hand, a cardinal theme. On a daily basis, the data we share enables others to keep track of what we are doing, to discover our preferences and beliefs, and to understand the essence of who we are. A familiar example is the number of Facebook "likes": the more likes a user gives, the better Facebook knows you—perhaps better than your colleague, better than your roommate, even better than your parents or children, and, in the event of 300 likes, maybe even better than your partner.[1] The next step seems only logical: the algorithm knows us better than we know ourselves. The same happens with data trails we leave on search engines: they allow others to fathom our identity.[2] Once others are knowledgeable about who we are, they may use this knowledge in either a benevolent or malicious manner. Hence, privacy matters, and so does the governance of privacy.

On the other hand, the concept of privacy already existed in the old, pre-Web world, though had a more particular meaning: 'the claim of individuals, groups, or institutions to determine for themselves when, how, and to what extent information about them is communicated to others' (I cite this definition from a 1967 discourse on privacy).[3]

1   Youyou, W., Kosinski, M., and Stillwell, D. (2015). Computers judge personalities better than humans. *Proceedings of the National Academy of Sciences*, 112(4), pp. 1036–1040.

2   Stephens-Davidowitz, S. (2017). *Everybody Lies*, New York: Dey Street Books.

3   Westin A. F. (1967). *Privacy and freedom*, New York: Atheneum.

Pre-Web definitions of privacy often contain three core elements: (1) individuals, (2) the control of their personal information, and (3) the right to be left alone.[4] However, in a data-driven world, privacy and the violation thereof have gained an entirely different meaning:

- Invasions of privacy entail more than just disclosure. In the world of data, algorithms, and artificial intelligence, data can be used to profile, intimidate or manipulate individual users. Profiling may also concern groups, which means that privacy violations do not only lead to individual damage, but also to collective damage. I will elaborate on this phenomenon later in this chapter.

- Privacy breaches are often data-based, while in the pre-Web world they mainly concerned information. A single data point often comes without any meaning[5]—data characterized as 'know-nothing'.[6] This may have a host of effects that are relevant to governance—for example, the mere fact that users perceive data as meaningless dots can make them less alert to possible privacy invasions.

- When data is being collected, a service is often rendered in return, such as medical care, online education, tailored search results. These services are often free of charge, and users pay with their data. The more that users value these services, the more privacy becomes part of a complicated trade-off, an essential difference from the pre-Web world. In the pre-Web world, privacy was about restricting the flow of information; in a data-driven world privacy is about ensuring that the information 'flows appropriately'.[7]

4   Becker, M. (2019). Privacy in the digital age: comparing and contrasting individual versus social approaches towards privacy. *Ethics and Information Technology, 21*, pp. 307–317.

5   Rowley, J., and Farrow, J. (2000). *Organizing knowledge: an introduction to managing access to information* (3rd Ed.), Aldershot: Gower.

6   Zeleny, M. (1987). Management Support Systems: Towards Integrated Knowledge Management. *Human Systems Management, 7*(1), pp. 59–70.

7   Nissenbaum, H. (2015). Respect for context as a benchmark for privacy online: What it is and isn't? In B. Roessler and D. Mokrosinska (Eds.), *Social Dimensions*

- Privacy is an all-encompassing concept. It involves everybody, and it affects almost anything—nearly everything in life has an online aspect. In the old world, the problem of violations of privacy often had a more limited scope. The issue of privacy has taken such a quantum leap that, at least from a governance perspective, it has become fundamentally different from what it once was.

These observations explain my initial discomfort with the title of this book. Using an old concept to describe a new phenomenon might be misleading. Privacy has developed beyond the pre-Web meaning of 'individual', 'control', and 'leaving alone'. However, the concept of privacy has become so commonplace that I cannot evade using it. But let us be clear: privacy is a much more layered concept than it was in pre-Web times. In this chapter, I will peel back these layers. Section 2 contains a few introductory remarks about privacy. In Sections 3–6 I will introduce four types of privacy invasions, which will then be compared in Section 7.

1.2 Privacy as a process (I)

The traditional concept of privacy can be visualized with the image of "my-home-is-my-castle": there is a territory which, in principle, no other person is allowed to enter.[8] The residents of the castle have a right to secrecy and control with secrecy having one clear meaning: what happens in my castle stays in my castle. Accordingly, control has an unambiguous meaning: the residents decide which information may leave the castle. When information stays behind the walls, there is privacy. When information leaves the castle without consent, there is a breach of privacy.

of Privacy: Interdisciplinary Perspectives (pp. 278–302). Cambridge: Cambridge University Press.

8   Stalder, F. (2002). Privacy is not the Antidote to Surveillance. *Surveillance and Society*, *1*(1), pp. 120–124.

Privacy as a dynamic and fluid concept

The castle metaphor is static—it is the image of an enclosed environment. Current privacy challenges are much more dynamic and can be visualized through the metaphor of the flow, the stream, or the journey—I will use these metaphors interchangeably in this book.

After data leaves an actor, data travels to other data and other actors. In some cases, the journey is very short; in other cases, the journey is long and unpredictable—it is not known in advance which data will be connected and whether these connections will have any effect on privacy. Privacy is therefore a process—a privacy invasion arises and builds up during this process. Privacy protection is less about fencing off an imaginary space (the castle walls) and more about protection against the excesses of the data flow.

The data-journey may start in several ways: with commercial transactions (transaction data), with visiting websites, with the use of devices that are linked to the Internet, by entering a public space with cameras (engagement data), through social media or by answering website feedback questions (attitudinal data), and, of course, users often have to leave personal data if they want to use Internet services.

Solove summarizes the process in four steps: data is (1) collected, (2) processed, (3) disseminated, and these three steps might eventually result in (4) a privacy invasion.[9] Privacy is, therefore, not a static, binary concept (information is inside or outside the castle)—it is a dynamic, fluid concept.

Continuous, non-linear, and unpredictable processes

The four steps, from data collection to privacy invasion, may suggest that privacy invasions are linear processes, which, of course,

9   Solove, D. J. (2006). A Taxonomy of Privacy. *University of Pennsylvania Law Review*, 154, pp. 477–560.

is not the case. Privacy as process can have several important additional features.

First, the process is a continuous one: data is continuously harvested and, continually, new data travels from the user, is processed and disseminated, and needs to be protected. That is why the metaphor of the stream is a powerful one: a stream continues to flow, albeit with a different intensity and in different directions.

Second, both at the individual and collective level, there are many data-journeys and these journeys take place simultaneously. The data-journeys are interconnected, which evokes the image of a spaghetti-like system. There are many spaghetti strands (the data-journeys), some of which are stuck together, so that data can jump from one strand to the other. There is an important consequence of this "spaghetti": the data-journeys are non-linear, no one can oversee them, and no one knows how they interfere

Third, the process of data collection itself can result in a privacy invasion, but that is not always the case. Data collection, processing, and dissemination can also lead to results that are positively valued: better service delivery, better education, or better health care. As a result of this, a privacy invasion is a process with uncertainty and unpredictability as a main feature. At the start of the journey, it is not always clear whether data collection will finally result in an invasion—not only because we do not know how the data dots will be connected, but also because the trade-off between privacy and other values may change during the process. If we learn during the journey that certain data make a much greater contribution to health than we initially thought, this can influence our views considering the trade-off between privacy and health.

In short, privacy is a process and privacy invasion is a process. This means that privacy invasion is in many cases a wicked problem:

– The factual question, "how does data travel; how does the journey go?" is often a difficult question to answer due to the spaghetti-like structure of the data-journeys.

– The moral question, is data being misused for a privacy violation or is it being used well for a valuable service? does not always have an unambiguous answer.

When a problem comes with both factual and moral uncertainties, it is called 'wicked'.[10] If the facts are clear and there is consensus about the moral dimension, there is a 'structured problem'. A privacy invasion can be a very structured problem. Posting revenge porn, not properly protecting credit card data, careless handling of patient data—we all agree that these data and privacy breaches are morally wrong. If the facts are clear (we know who made the mistake or who is responsible for the mistake) and we agree about the values and norms (the mistake is morally wrong) then the invasion is a structured problem. However, in this book I want to cover the full complexity of the problem of privacy invasions, which are largely wicked.

Principles of data-protection

There are a number of important principles and rules to protect users' data and privacy. These principles can, for instance, be found in Article 5.1 of the European Union's General Data Protection Regulation (GDPR); see the box below.

Personal data shall be:
(a) processed lawfully, fairly and in a transparent manner in relation to individuals ('lawfulness, fairness, and transparency');
(b) collected for specified, explicit, and legitimate purposes and not further processed in a manner that is incompatible with those purposes; further processing for archiving purposes in the public interest, scientific or historical research purposes, or statistical

10 Alford, J., and Head, B. W. (2017). Wicked and less wicked problems: a typology and a contingency framework. *Policy and Society*, *36*(3), pp. 397–413, doi: 10.1080/14494035.2017.1361634.

purposes shall […] not be considered to be incompatible with the initial purposes ('purpose limitation');

(c) adequate, relevant and limited to what is necessary in relation to the purposes for which they are processed ('data minimization');

(d) accurate and, where necessary, kept up to date; every reasonable step must be taken to ensure that personal data that are inaccurate, having regard to the purposes for which they are processed, are erased or rectified without delay ('accuracy');

(e) kept in a form which permits identification of data subjects for no longer than is necessary for the purposes for which the personal data are processed; personal data may be stored for longer periods insofar as the personal data will be processed solely for archiving purposes in the public interest, scientific or historical research purposes or statistical purposes […] subject to the implementation of the appropriate technical and organizational measures required by the GDPR to safeguard the rights and freedoms of individuals ('storage limitation');

(f) processed in a manner that ensures appropriate security of the personal data, including protection against unauthorized or unlawful processing and accidental loss, destruction or damage, using appropriate technical or organizational measures ('integrity and confidentiality').

Source: Regulation (EU) 2016/679 of the European Parliament and the Council, General Data Protection regulation

Regulations such as the GDPR offer strong protection of data and privacy. The GDPR's principles bind data collection and without these principles there is no data protection. However, the principles are always related to a purpose, and therefore require a trade-off between data collection and that purpose. If data collection purposes are fixed and unambiguous at the start of the data-journey, a singular trade-off can be made. If the purpose changes, or the purpose is ambiguous or perceptions of the purpose change, the trade-off might change over time. Privacy is a process and the application of the principles is often a process too.

Data use and privacy

There are two possible views on the relationship between data use and privacy violations.[11] The first implies that a data breach is equivalent to a privacy violation. When someone's data falls into the hands of a third party in an improper manner, that person's privacy is violated; therefore, a data breach=privacy breach. The second view is that processing data is permitted—there is only a privacy breach when data is misused later on, during the data-journey.

Without taking a position in this discussion, the distinction between data breaches and privacy breaches is relevant from a governance perspective. There are at least two reasons for this:

– A privacy breach is a process: a data breach takes place and later has certain consequences. From a process perspective, the distinction between data breach and privacy breach matters. Why? Because this process is often non-linear and can be very unpredictable: (I) the major privacy breach can be the result of a series of minor data breaches; (II) normative views on privacy versus other values either will or will not change during the process—what appeared to be a privacy breach may not prove to be a privacy breach after all, and vice versa; (III) it is even conceivable that a privacy breach takes place without being preceded by a formal data breach. There are other examples, but what matters here is that these different types of processes, from data breach to privacy breach, can require different types of governance. So, from a governance perspective, the difference between data breach and privacy breach is very relevant.

– There is always the issue of capacity. Suppose that data breach A leads to a low-impact privacy breach and data breach B leads to a high-impact privacy breach. Suppose that a regulator belongs to the school of "data breach=privacy

11   Bygrave, L.A. (2017). Data protection by Design and by Default: Deciphering the EU's Legislative Requirements. *Oslo Law Review, 4*(2), pp. 105–120. But, for the EU, see: Kokott, J., and Sobotta, C. (2013). The distinction between privacy and data protection in the jurisprudence of the CJEU and the ECtHR. *International Data Privacy Law, 3*(4), pp. 222–228.

breach". Therefore, according to this regulator, there is a privacy breach in both cases. Nevertheless, this regulator will consider the difference between A and B: every regulator has limited capacity and must select those breaches that will be dealt with. Low-impact cases will be given a low priority. A regulator may define a data breach as a privacy breach but will nevertheless use the distinction between data and privacy breach when making decisions regarding priorities.

There is, undoubtedly, more to mention, but first I will further peel back the concept of privacy. The starting point is the traditional concept of privacy: "my home is my castle". In the world of data and the Internet, privacy is a layered phenomenon and at least four types of privacy can be added to pre-Web privacy concept.

1.3 Type 1: privacy invasions as disclosure – continuous, ubiquitous, and emergent

A type 1 privacy invasion is, in large part, similar to traditional, my-home-is-my-castle invasions. But it is also different. It is similar because it also concerns the values of disclosure and secrecy. Information that is supposed to be private is disclosed to third parties. It is different because, on the Internet, private information is ubiquitous and is eternally retrievable. Two metaphors are helpful here: the earthquake and the dormant volcano—again, we will learn that privacy is a process.

The earthquake with aftershocks – privacy as an ongoing process

The well-known example here is revenge porn. A member of the US Congress has become the victim of revenge porn.[12] The

---

12   Hill, K. (2020). *She Will Rise. Becoming a Warrior in the Battle for True Equality*, New York: Grand Central Publishing. (p. 6).

pictures have been published by a website and a tabloid and immediately go viral. Social media such as Facebook and YouTube deploy their anti-revenge porn policies and remove the photos, but this is in no way sufficient to prevent further distribution. These photos would end up in a tabloid in the pre-Web world and would only be seen by a limited readership—today, they are always retrievable, and can be retrieved by anyone.

As such, a privacy violation is no longer a one-time shock—the making public of photos that will slowly disappear from collective memory—and may be a lifelong process, with many painful aftershocks. Time and time again the images can re-emerge. Just like an earthquake, a shock can be followed by aftershocks, which may be even heavier than the actual earthquake itself. The victim does not know when these aftershocks will present themselves, and the fear of these aftershocks may sometimes be greater than the aftershock itself. In Section 2, I refer to Solove's summary of privacy as a process: data collection, processing, and dissemination may eventually result in a privacy invasion. The metaphor of the earthquake makes clear that a privacy invasion is not just the endpoint of the data-journey, it is also a process—an ongoing process, not a one-time affair.

The dormant volcano – privacy as an emergent process

Violations of privacy can present themselves in a wholly unexpected manner: what is harmless today may prove to be a privacy violation tomorrow.

- Information may be re-adapted. In 2019 it was discovered that a 'softcore paedophile ring' was copying and editing innocuous YouTube clips of children.[13] Members used a timestamp to indicate when children unintentionally adopt a particular

---

13   Watson, M. (2019). *YouTube is Facilitating the Sexual Exploitation of Children, and it's Being Monetized*, https://www.youtube.com/watch?v=O13G5A5w5P0; Boderick, R. (February 22, 2019). *YouTube's Latest Child Controversy Has Kick-Started A War Over How To Fix The Platform*, BuzzFeed.News.

pose. The pieces of these videos were then pasted together and distributed among a network of YouTube commenters. Initially innocent pictures—children who are engaging in sports or dancing—are suddenly abused by third parties. An innocent picture of today may result in a severe privacy violation tomorrow.

- Subsequently, there is the phenomenon of re-contextualization. Twenty years ago, a person may have appeared in a video that was posted online by someone else; it is just one of the many videos on the Web. Suppose this person is a visible public figure today and the video suddenly attracts attention—maybe the person said a few things in a private context that are problematic in today's public realm. In the current context, the twenty year old post has suddenly become a privacy breach. Another example can be seen in "sharenting", where parents share information about their children on social media. Today, it is nice and cute, but tomorrow it might be used for building digital dossiers on the children.[14]

- Technological dynamics may lead to privacy violations. For many video makers, TikTok clips are a harmless form of leisure. Often, the makers are fully visual, with their faces being visible. Consider a thought experiment: imagine that, with the development of facial recognition, TikTok clips could be used to gather biometric data of individuals. That would be significantly less harmless.

In essence: information that is currently more or less harmless may become a privacy breach in the future. Here, the metaphor that can be used is that of a volcanic eruption: the volcano lies dormant, but the dangerous eruption may manifest at a moment's notice. Likewise, privacy invasion is not just a process, but an emergent process—the invasion can suddenly pop up.

14   Plunkett, A. L. (2019). *Sharenthood: Why We Should Think before We Talk About Our Kids Online*, Boston: MIT Press.

1.4 Type 2: privacy invasions as profiling

In the transition from type 1 to type 2, the concept of privacy changes fundamentally. Information is not disclosed, instead, users are profiled.

Data-based profiling

Primarily: using services is relinquishing data—and this data can then be used to profile individuals. In many cases, booking hotel rooms on a website is the same as building a profile, based on preferences for locations, timeframes, types of hotels, or group size. This is, again, relatively harmless, but things may get out of hand. In computer science literature, one research is published after the other, showing how, with a limited dataset, quite detailed user profiles can be created.[15]

Often, the message of the research is that with (1) 'easily accessible digital records of behaviour' (2), analysts can give an accurate prediction of (3) 'highly sensitive personal attributes including: sexual orientation, ethnicity, religious and political views, personality traits, intelligence, happiness, use of addictive substances, parental separation, age, and gender.'[16]

Examples of data or meta-data that may be used to build profiles are:
- Data concerning search behaviour—keywords may provide an insight into a person's age, gender, and political and religious identity;[17]

---

15   Privacy International (n. d.). *Examples of Data Points Used in Profiling*, privacyinternational.org.

16   Kosinski, M., Stillwell, D., and Graepel, T. (2013). Private traits and attributes are predictable from digital records of human behavior. *Proceedings of the National Academy of Sciences, 110*(15), pp. 5802–5805.

17   Bi, B., Shokouhi, M., Kosinski, M., and Graepel, T. (2013). Inferring the demographics of search users: Social data meets search queries. In *Proceedings of the 22nd international conference on World Wide Web*, pp. 131–140.

- Mobile phone meta-data—conclusions may be drawn about a person's wealth from the volume, mobility, and structure of their contact network;[18]
- Data about keystroke dynamics— the rhythm of typing patterns on a standard keyboard can be used to determine user emotion;[19]
- Instagram pictures—researchers claim that, based on Instagram pictures, they are able to make a reasonable prediction as to whether an individual has depression;[20]
- Smartphone meta-data—the number of calls a person makes per day or night, and their daily smartphone use can be used to predict a person's personality traits.[21]

All kinds of data may be used to procure a profile: input data (data that users have given about themselves), observed data (data based on observations about what users occupy themselves with), and reputation data (data concerning other people's perception of a person, such as their client rating or likes), as well as inferred data, which is constructed by analysts. With a considerable volume of this data, the focus lies in content-driven data footprints (e.g., likes), but meta-data may also lead to profound profiling of individual users.

18   Blumenstock, J., Cadamuro, G., and On, R. (2015). Predicting poverty and wealth from mobile phone metadata. *Science, 350*(6264), pp.1073–1076.
19   Epp, C., Lippold, M., and Mandryk, R. L. (2011). Identifying emotional states using keystroke dynamics, *Proceedings of the SIGCHI Conference on Human Factors in Computing Systems*, pp. 715–724.
20   Tufekci, Z. (April 21, 2019). *Think You're Discreet Online? Think Again*, The New York Times.
21   Stachl, C., Au, Q., Schoedel, R., Gosling, S. D., Harari, G. M., Buschek, D., Völkel, S. T., Schuwerk, T., Oldemeier, M., Ullmann, T., Hussmann, H., Bischl, B., and Bühner, M. (2020). Predicting personality from patterns of behavior collected with smartphones. *Proceedings of the National Academy of Sciences, 117*(30), pp. 17680–17687, doi: 10.1073/pnas.1920484117.

Profiling using other people's data

In the examples above, users provide data dots, but, as stated above, a user's profile can be created based on data shared by their fellow users. Users have data and information on other users—contact lists, the results of online competitions, all kinds of interactions—and can share that information with third parties.

Co-users may exchange data, allowing analysts to make group profiles. For instance, a group of users may be characterized by A, B, C, D, and E. Suppose that several users in this group fanatically shield their data about E, and in no way relinquish these data, but that analysts do possess their data for A, B, C, and D. Under certain conditions, an analyst may predict what E entails for these users with a near-certain probability; they can do this because the analyst has the data about E that concerns other members of the group. The data dots are like a trail of breadcrumbs—they lead to information about an individual user. The fact that a single crumb is missing is of no consequence whatsoever.

Profile amplification

There is also the phenomenon of profile amplification, where data from a limited group of users is harvested in order to profile big groups of other users. I will give an example that is partly based on the Cambridge Analytica scandal in 2018.
- Researchers invite a group of respondents to participate in, for example, a personality test, which results in an OCEAN score—a score related to the dimensions Openness, Conscientiousness, Extraversion, Agreeableness, and Neuroticism.
- Thereafter, the results of the personality test are linked to specific data—for instance, respondents' likes on Facebook or smartphone usage logs.
- The researchers will look for patterns and subsequently build algorithms, which can predict characteristics based on, for instance, a person's likes.

- Subsequently, the likes of the second group of respondents are collected and, with the help of the algorithm, the respondents' OCEAN scores are predicted. These respondents are also asked to fill in the personality test to check whether or not the likes predicted their scores correctly. The outcomes are used to perfect the algorithm.
- Of course, this process can be repeated several times. When successful, it means that a user "only" leaves data in the form of likes but that an algorithm exists that may, with the support of these likes, predict that user's personality.

The example shows how relatively easy it is to create an amplifier; a small group of respondents is thoroughly researched to give meaning to the data they relinquish. Subsequently, analysts can make far-reaching statements about large groups of other users based on limited datasets.

Furthermore, we need to bear in mind that individuals can be profiled incorrectly or linked to the wrong group. For example, a person may be allocated to a specific user category that is given a profile, but that person belongs within the 10% where the profile is not applicable. However, an incorrect profile can also invade privacy—I will return to this in the next section.

Data collection and profiling as sequential or parallel processes

Finally, it is essential to distinguish between data collection and profiling as sequential processes and data collection and profiling as parallel processes.

Sequential. Suppose a person regularly books a hotel via a website. In doing so, the user leaves a data trail, which the service provider may subsequently use for profiling.

- There is, based on the latter, a clear division between (a) providing services (booking the hotel), (b) data gathering (collecting the most vital data about the hotel bookings), and (c) subsequent profiling (using the collection of data to create a user profile).

- Providing services, data gathering, and profiling are sequential activities—initially, there is the provision of services, then there is data gathering, and, after that, a profile is determined. Of course, this is a continuous process, but this does not diminish its sequential character.

Conversely, there are types of online services, where,

- providing services, gathering data, and creating a profile are fully integrated;
- thus, service provision, collecting data, and profiling are parallel activities—they are performed simultaneously.

A few examples of these services:

- Advice about nutritional supplements. Advice about nutritional supplements will be based on data about a person's lifestyle, medical information, goals, and personal values. An algorithm assembles a package of nutritional supplements, users report their progression (muscle growth, sleeping patterns), and, subsequently, the composition of the package can be further refined.
- Styling advice. An online shop may provide styling advice based on data the user shares. Subsequently, an algorithm suggests suitable clothing to the user. The user is required to rate suggestions and, after that, a new suggestion—this continues until the user is happy.
- Advice about information. Users are offered tailored online magazines with themes within their particular interest. Again, a user relinquishes data and an algorithm creates a magazine that is in line with the interests of the user. Data about reading behaviour may subsequently be used to fine-tune the magazine.

In cases such as these, profiling is a *sine qua non* for the service provision—without profiling, there can be no provision of services. From the perspective of governance, this is an important observation. A hotel booking site can also perform without profiling and so, from the perspective of governance, there are possibilities to rein in data collection. When profiling is a *sine qua non* for service provision, this may be much more difficult, and data protection may lead to termination of the service.

To summarize: how does a type 2 privacy invasion relate to the traditional concept of privacy?

- As opposed to the traditional violation of privacy, data and information are used to profile and not to disclose. Companies who create a profile of a user often benefit from keeping this information hidden since it is strategic business information. This profile may be extraordinarily detailed, and may also concern users who have given no or limited data.
- With a traditional privacy violation, the focus lies on information rather than data—a type 2 breach involves data that has been translated into information.
- The traditional privacy violation is, generally, a momentary phenomenon; a type 2 privacy violation is a continuous process—a profile is created, and profiles are refined or adjusted with new data. Life is a journey, and our profile will travel along with us as a digital shadow. When we change, our digital shadow changes accordingly.

1.5   Type 3: privacy invasion as manipulation

Profiles may be used to influence individual users;[22] here, users receive particular information about specific products or services in line with their profile, which might be in the interest of both the service provider and the user.

---

22   Stalder, F. (2002). Privacy is not the Antidote to Surveillance. *Surveillance and Society*, *1*(1), pp. 120–124.

Information – selective information – manipulation

But there is more. Informing may grow into selective informing and, subsequently, into intimidation or manipulation. The
more precise the profile, the more precisely this intimidation or
manipulation can be designed.

-   In the world of products and services, profiling may imply
    that some users are to receive an offer that is not presented
    to other users. This is efficient and effective, but it may also
    develop into manipulation: users with a particular profile
    are not offered houses in specific areas or may have a harder
    time getting a loan.[23]
-   A similar phenomenon can occur in the world of ideas.
    For example, one user is shown a political advert, another
    user does not receive the advert. Since this microtargeting
    enables attuning the advert to a certain profile, manipulation
    looms. During the Brexit referendum, the Leave campaign
    bombarded constituents with specific profiles with adverts
    that often contained controversial claims.[24] Voters who care
    about animal rights were given an advert with the following
    text: 'The EU is supporting commercial whaling by forc-
    ing us to allow ships carrying whale meat to dock in our
    ports!'—while, in reality, the EU does not support commercial
    whaling.
-   In addition to this, users have certain beliefs, including
    underlying preconceptions and biases. These beliefs can

23   Benjamin, R. (2019). *Race After Technology: Abolitionist Tools for the New Jim Code*, Cambridge: Polity Press.; Williams, B. A., Brooks, C. F., and Shmargad, Y. (2018). How Algorithms Discriminate Based on Data They Lack: Challenges, Solutions, and Policy Implications. *Journal of Information Policy, 8*, pp. 78–115.; Schneider, V. (2020). Locked Out by Big Data: How Big Data, Algorithms and Machine Learning May Undermine Housing Justice. *Columbia Human Rights Law Review, 52*(1), pp. 251–305.
24   Cadwalladr, C. (May 7, 2017). The great British Brexit robbery: how our de-mocracy was hijacked, *The Observer*.; Sebastão, D., and Borges, S. (2021). Should we stay or should we go: EU input legitimacy under threat? Social media and Brexit. *Transforming Government, People, Process and Policy, 15*(3), pp. 335–346.

be part of their profile, which means that they constantly receive information confirming those beliefs, preconceptions, and biases. Again, this may grow into manipulation. I will address this more extensively in Chapter 6.

– The more data a malicious party has that concerns an individual, the better that individual can be profiled—and the more ingeniously a phishing-email can be constructed. Furthermore, think of "doxing"—private data is collected to create a profile (a "doc"). Subsequently, the doxed person can be intimidated in all kinds of ways—through anonymous threats, via a social media call to threaten that person, or by buying goods in online stores on behalf of the person who has been doxed.

The digital identity overrules the "real" identity

What we see here is, again, privacy invasion as a process: harvesting data—profiling users—offering tailored information to users—influencing users—manipulating and intimidating them. The next step may be the digital profile overruling the user themselves, thereby superseding who a person truly is.

Analytically, we can distinguish between a digital identity or profile and a "real identity". A person's real identity can never be fully objectified, allows different interpretations, and is ambiguous and fluid. A digital identity is often much more conclusive—the algorithm provides a particular personal credit score or awards a person with certain characteristics. Such scores may differ, greatly or not, from someone's "real identity".

If (1) a digital identity strongly deviates from a real identity and (2) many decisions are based on digital profiles, there is a significant risk: someone's digital identity will rule over the real identity or, in other words, one becomes the captive of their digital identity.[25]

---

25   See for example: Eubanks, V. (2018). *Automating Inequality*, New York: St. Martin's Press.; Benjamin, R. (2019). *Race After Technology: Abolitionist Tools for*

This process may be harmless or even fun. For example, you are traveling and end up in a hideous village in the middle of nowhere. The algorithm thinks that this is the place to be for you, incorporates this in your profile, and subsequently bombards you with offers of hotels in the village. But it can also be quite serious: credit may be denied or a person may have no access to particular information since their underlying digital profile is not in line with their real profile. It seems to be good news when data collection and processing results in an incorrect profile: the data did not reveal a user's identity. But it is also bad news: an incorrectly profiled user may be intimidated or manipulated because of this incorrect profile.

Profiling and manipulation as parallel processes

With type 2 privacy violations, providing services and relinquishing data may run in a sequential and parallel fashion (see Section 4). A sequential process means that a user buys a service and, as such, leaves data. Data follows services. The service provider may subsequently use the data—for instance, to provide a better offer next time. A parallel process means that the relinquishing of data is an integral part of the service provision—remember the example of styling advice. It is not "data follows services", but "data defines the service".

The distinction between sequential and parallel is also relevant for type 3 privacy invasions. Sequential means that there is a profile and that, subsequently, someone tries to manipulate the profiled user. Parallel means that manipulation is also used to construct someone's profile. When someone has a profile that makes them sensitive to, for example, 9/11 conspiracy theories, the possibility exists that the user will be continuously targeted with information about conspiracies. It is not just a person's profile, which is later used to manipulate ("manipulation follows profiling")—manipulation also creates a profile.

the New Jim Code, Cambridge: Polity Press.

To sum up, how, then, does the type 3 violation relate to the traditional concept of privacy?

–   Different from the traditional violation of privacy, data and information are used to inform and manipulate individuals by using their profile, which is based on the data they have shared.
–   The relation between profile and manipulation is reciprocal: a profile is being used to manipulate, and this manipulation influences a person's profile.
–   This means that a type 3 violation is nearing a reversal of the traditional concept of privacy. A traditional privacy invasion means that personal information is moving to a third party, outside the castle—it is an inside-out movement. Here, the action goes the other way round: the third party disposes of my personal information and uses it to influence me—an outside-in action. What is even more egregious, the third party possesses information about me that I do not possess.
–   In this case too we see that privacy violation is a process. There is a chain from profiling to manipulation, profiles are continually being renewed, and new opportunities to inform and manipulate are continually being developed.

1.6   Type 4: privacy invasion as a collective problem

Thus far, the individual user has been the victim of the aforementioned kinds of privacy violations.

Data is used to profile individual users (type 2) and subsequently to inform them—or to manipulate and intimidate them (type 3).

From the individual to the collective level

A type 4 privacy violation happens when the focus shifts from the individual to the collective level—to groups or communities, or even to society as a whole. Often, type 3 violations automatically lead to type 4 privacy violations: when algorithms lead to discrimination of profiled users in the housing or the job market, it not only affects individuals, but entire groups and, ultimately, society as a whole—the soul of an entire country. If an algorithm delivers fake news to users of a particular profile, and if this happens on a large scale, this does not only affect these individuals, but it may deepen societal divides or foster distrust of existing institutions (government, science, the legal system). A significant effect may also be the blurring of the boundary between what is fake and what is fact, between truth and untruth—and type 4 privacy invasions might result in corrosion at the very fundament of a society.

Grouping profiled users

Furthermore, individual digital identities may be used to distinguish particular groups of users—from Facebook's refined typology of customers to groups of inspectees created by inspection agencies. Grouping profiled users comes with a variety of risks: an individual can get the wrong profile, end up in the wrong group, or assumptions about the preferences and behaviour of a group may be incorrect.

If (1) groups are a tool for powerful actors (e.g., government agencies, monopolists in the market) and (2) one or more of these risks manifest themselves this might result in abuse of power. Each country has iconic examples of groups who have fallen victim to governmental bureaucracies, using group profiles to impose their policies.

Privacy is a process. Upstream, there is data collection. Midstream, data is used to profile and manipulate individuals, which can have a significant and negative impact downstream, on groups or society as a whole. A well-known warning by Shoshana Zuboff states that the accumulation of personal data can lead to 'surveillance capitalism' that 'threatens the existential and political canon of the modern liberal order defined by principles of self-determination'.[26]

As I said in the Introduction, privacy violations in a data-driven world are fundamentally different from pre-Web privacy violations. A type 4 violation is a complete reversal of the traditional concept of privacy.

- A pre-Web violation of privacy deals with disclosure, a type 4 privacy invasion deals with manipulation and intimidation. 'My home is my castle' is the summary of pre-Web privacy. Disclosure means that information leaves the castle; intimidation and manipulation mean that information enters the castle.
- A pre-Web violation of privacy implies that the individual is the victim. In our data-driven world, individual privacy violations can be amplified, which can have far-reaching consequences for the collective—a community or society as a whole.

Figure 1.1 provides an overview of this development. A type 1 privacy violation most closely resembles a traditional privacy violation. Information about an individual is exposed, and the movement is inside out.

A type 2 privacy invasion is about profiling. Profiles are partly built with information about the individual (inside out) and partly with external information (outside in); think of the example of Cambridge Analytica or the use of publicly available data to refine a profile.

In the case of type 3 privacy invasions, the profile is used to inform or manipulate individuals—the outside-in movement. Ultimately, it not only has consequences for individuals but also for the collective (type 4).

---

26   Zuboff, S. (2015). Big Other: Surveillance Capitalism and the Prospects of an Information Civilization. *Journal of Information Technology, 30*(1), pp. 75–89.; Zuboff, S. (March 5, 2016). *The Secrets of Surveillance Capitalism*, Frankfurter Allgemeine Zeitung.

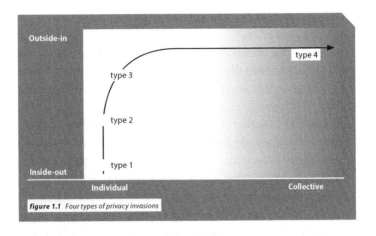

figure 1.1 *Four types of privacy invasions*

1.7 Privacy as a process (II): comparing the four types of privacy invasions

Figure 1.2 offers an overview of the most relevant differences between the four types of privacy and privacy violations.

The first three lines of the Figure have been addressed extensively. There are the movements from information to data, from disclosure to manipulation, and from individual to collective victims.

The next distinction: a pre-Web privacy violation is much more of a one-time event, and type 1 to 4 privacy violations are more of a process.

Privacy as a process indicates a data-journey or a data stream, which begins with collecting and processing information and can eventually result in a privacy invasion.[27] This process has three additional characteristics:

- The privacy invasion as a continuous process. Information is stored on the web in perpetuity (such as revenge porn, type 1) and a continuous stream of data dots are connected—as

27   Solove, D. J. (2006). A Taxonomy of Privacy. *University of Pennsylvania Law Review, 154,* pp. 477–560.

Pre-Web	Type 1	Type 2	Type 3	Type 4
Predominantly information	Data and information	Data	Data	Data
Disclosure	Disclosure and (re)construction	Profiling	Manipulating	Manipulating
Individual	Individual	Individual	Individual	Collective
Moment	Process	Process	Process	Process
Linear	Linear	Non-linear	Non-linear	Non-linear

figure 1.2 *Types of privacy invasions: a comparison*

such, a constant process of profiling and influencing happens (types 2, 3, and 4).

– The privacy invasion as an emergent process. I addressed emergence earlier with type 1 privacy violations—the harmless information of today may result in a privacy violation tomorrow. But emergence is also crucial in type 2–4 violations. Here, seemingly meaningless data dots exist, but from a collection of data dots emerges a profile (type 2), which may be used for manipulation (type 3), something resulting in far-reaching societal consequences (type 4).

– The privacy invasion as a non-linear process. The image of the data-journey may be deceiving—it suggests that there is a linear process, as if data travels from A to B. In addressing type 2–4 violations, it was indicated that these processes are, in fact, non-linear; data collection, profiling, and influencing are parallel and capricious processes within a spaghetti-like network.

The governance of privacy

This book focuses on the role governments can play in protecting privacy. I define the governance of privacy as 'the instruments and strategies that governments can use to protect their citizen's privacy'. This definition is based on Lynn, Heinrich, and Hill, who define governance as the 'regimes, laws, rules, judicial decisions, and administrative practices that constrain, prescribe, and enable the provision of publicly supported goals and services'.[28] There are two distinctions to this definition: (1) the 'publicly supported goals and services' are, of course, more specific; this book is about privacy, and (2) Lynn, Heinrich, and Hill seem to refer mainly to legal instruments, but there are also other instruments that can be used for privacy protection (see Chapter 3).

Privacy as a process has significant consequences for governance: it provides both opportunities and limitations for privacy governance. Privacy as process offers opportunities for governance. When data travels, there are many more moments of opportunity to interrupt the journey than when a privacy breach is a one-time affair. In the language of the data stream: if upstream interventions fail, there still are opportunities to intervene downstream.

Privacy as a process also creates limitations for governance— the totality of non-linear processes provides a very capricious image of all the data-journeys, which overlap in a range of particular moments. Again, the image of a spaghetti-like structure comes to mind, which admittedly is very hard to get a grip on. The next chapter provides a more detailed analysis of the complexity of the governance challenge.

28   Lynn Jr., L. E., Heinrich, C. J., and Hill, C. J. (2001). Improving Governance: A New Logic for Empirical Research, Washington DC: Georgetown University Press.

2   The Complexity of the Governance Challenge

2.1   Introduction

How can the value of privacy be safeguarded? What can governments do, directly or indirectly? Before these questions can be answered, I will need to explore the complexity of the governance challenge. In the following chapters, I will discuss strategies for safeguarding privacy, and these strategies will only be effective if they meet this complexity head on.

To outline this complexity, I will revisit the pre-Web "my home is my castle" metaphor. Imagine the castle's residents are being harassed by paparazzi, who take pictures of what goes on behind the castle walls. The images are subsequently published in a tabloid, which is an invasion of the residents' privacy. This invasion emerges in a chain of actors and factors:[1]

- There is a victim: the residents of the castle. Their private information is being made public without their consent.
- There are objects with which the privacy violation is materialized. In this example, there are two objects—the picture and the tabloid.
- The objects are produced by several devices. The picture is taken with a camera before being developed and printed in a darkroom, the tabloid is then multiplied using a printing press.
- Hidden behind the devices are the villains who have caused the privacy violation itself—the photographer and the tabloid editors. Possibly, there are other villains—the tabloid's publisher and the distributor.

---

1   In part, I borrow these concepts from Helen Nissenbaum, although she uses them within a different context. Nissenbaum, H. (2010). *Privacy in Context: Technology, Policy and the Integrity of Social Life*, Palo Alto: Stanford University Press.

- There is a distribution process, as the tabloid must be transported to present it at its points of sale.
- There are the recipients or addressees, in the case of the photo these are the readers of the tabloid.

In Sections 2–7, I will use these six aspects of a privacy violation to describe the complexity of the challenges governments face in a data-driven world. For each of these aspects, the situation in a data-driven world is much more ambiguous than it was in the pre-Web world, which makes governance a complex challenge. Sections 8 and 9 summarize this complexity.

2.2 Victims and their many cost–benefit analyses

In a traditional privacy violation, there is a clear victim. Moreover, the potential victim has a strong interest in privacy protection since the damage of a breach can be substantial, and can result in public humiliation, financial harm, disrupted personal relationships, et cetera.

Perceived costs and benefits of data sharing

In the world of the Internet and privacy, the victim is often a more ambivalent phenomenon. The data and information leading to privacy violations are, by and large, relinquished by the victim in return for all kinds of services, from better search results to advice on healthy behaviour, from new friend networks to interesting itineraries. Figure 2.1 shows the perceived costs and benefits of sharing data.

The quadrants in Figure 2.1 show a variety of users, and only in quadrant II do we see an alert user. The users in quadrants I, III, and IV are much less alert, they are indifferent, hesitant, or even willing to relinquish data.

The Figure pertains not to "real" costs and benefits, but also to perceived costs and benefits, which may lead to an important

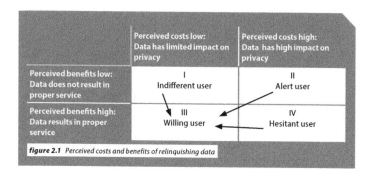

	Perceived costs low: Data has limited impact on privacy	Perceived costs high: Data has high impact on privacy
Perceived benefits low: Data does not result in proper service	I Indifferent user	II Alert user
Perceived benefits high: Data results in proper service	III Willing user	IV Hesitant user

figure 2.1 *Perceived costs and benefits of relinquishing data*

dynamic as indicated by the three arrows. After all, the service providers can influence these perceptions by overemphasizing the advantages of high-quality service delivery and by downplaying the disadvantages of possible privacy invasions. In addition, they can feed the perception that users receive high-end services by merely relinquishing a few data dots. This may lure users from quadrants I, II, and IV to quadrant III.

Complementing incentives for data sharing

There are three additional observations that are relevant here.[2] Several complementing mechanisms may feed the perception of high benefit and low cost. Again, the result is that users tend to end up in quadrant III of Figure 2.1.

First, the benefits of sharing data exist in the present; the costs lie in the future (see quadrant II in Figure 2.2.1). This may activate a "present bias" whereby immediate rewards are rated significantly higher than the consequences of a choice in the longer term. Service providers can exploit this bias by offering the illusion of control or by exploiting the user's impatience.[3]

2   Barth, S., and De Jong, M. D. (2017). The privacy paradox: Investigating discrepancies between expressed privacy concerns and actual online behavior—A systematic literature review. *Telematics and informatics, 34*(7), pp. 1038–1058.
3   John, L. K. (September 18, 2018). *Uninformed consent,* Harvard Business Review.

	Benefits now	Benefits later			Benefits visible	Benefits not visible			Individual benefits	Collective benefits
Costs now				Costs visible				Individual costs		
Costs later	Strong incentive to share data			Costs not visible	Strong incentive to share data			Collective costs	Strong incentive to share data	

figure 2.2.1
Costs and benefits of data sharing

figure 2.2.2

figure 2.2.3

Second, while the benefits of relinquishing data are visible and clear, the costs are not (see quadrant III in Figure 2.2.2). Data may be used for privacy invasions, but often this may not be the case. Data ends up on the bottom of the information ocean to remain there unused—at least, according to the users' perception—for eternity.

Third, the benefits of sharing data lie with the individual; the costs lie with the collective (see quadrant III in Figure 2.2.3). In Chapter 1, I addressed type 4 privacy violations, in which the damage of the privacy violation does not solely pertain to the individual but, rather, to society as a whole. In these type 4 violations, the costs lie mainly with the collective, and this may, again, provide an impetus for the individual user to hand over data.

Bias comes into play for each of the mechanisms in Figure 2.2. As said, there is the "present bias", but also the bias to overestimate the benefits and underestimate the costs.[4]

Of course, there are important nuances here. For example, there may be a user who is heavily dependent on benefits from a government and who must therefore give up a lot of personal data. This user may be a captive in quadrant IV of Figure 2.1;

4   Chen, H. T. (2018). Revisiting the privacy paradox on social media with an extended privacy calculus model: The effect of privacy concerns, privacy self-efficacy, and social capital on privacy management. *American Behavioral Scientist*, 62(10), pp.1392–1412.

here, the perceived cost is high, but so are the benefits because the user is highly dependent on the government. This hesitant user may not want to give up certain data but, as a captive user, cannot avoid the quadrant IV situation.[5]

In a data-driven world, people share data

Users who find themselves in quadrant III of Figure 2.1 (the willing users), and thus perceive high benefits and low costs, may also become desensitized in terms of the cost of potential loss of privacy. When you find yourself in quadrant III, it is quite a big step to acknowledge that the costs are much higher than had previously been perceived. As a result, even underlying normative beliefs about privacy may change. The idea might occur that sharing large amounts of data is inevitable in modern-day society and those who want to benefit from Web-based services will have to relinquish their data and compromise their privacy.

To summarize, we see that the victim is less clear than in the pre-Web world. Victims continuously give away data and information and, as such, continuously feed the possibilities for privacy violations. The ambivalence of the victim does not mean that the victim is guilty of privacy violation, nor does it diminish the responsibility of data recipients, who often exploit this ambivalence. The ambivalence only clarifies how complex the governance of privacy can be; the privacy of citizens must be protected but, at the same time, those citizens have strong incentives to hand over data.

2.3 The object: data and the many uncertainties concerning data use

The privacy violation in the pre-Web world is perpetrated with two objects: the photograph and the tabloid. The photograph is

---

5   Holderness, H. (2013). Taxing Privacy. *Georgetown Journal on Poverty Law & Policy*, *21*(1), pp. 1–41.

meaningful information—that is why the tabloid is interested in it. This may still be the case, as private photographs or recordings of private conversations can be posted on the Internet. In many cases, however, privacy violations are data-based and, as such, the object is a lot less unequivocal. Why?

Uncertainties: the metaphor of the mosaic

First and foremost, data is often a series of meaningless dots, which are stored somewhere, but which will forever remain meaningless. The process of sense-making will only begin then, when a number of these dots are connected and when data is being converted into information. The violation of privacy occurs in a process: (a) gathering data, (b) creating information by connecting the dots, and (c) subsequently using or misusing this information. This process involves several perceived uncertainties from the perspective of the user.

Uncertainty about sense-making. The process of "connecting the dots" might be quite unpredictable. Here, we can use the metaphor of a mosaic: from a vast number of small stones with a multitude of colours (data), an image emerges. Data dots are like these stones, and users are often not aware beforehand (1) which stones, (2) by whom, and (3) in what way will be used to make (4) a certain kind of mosaic. This can only be ascertained in hindsight once the mosaic is made. Consequently, users relinquish data but have no idea whatsoever whether this data will create information in the future, nor what information will be created. This applies to both data and metadata.[6]

Uncertainty about the use of information. When information is manufactured—when the mosaic is made—users are often unaware of whether and how this information will be used. Will it

---

6   Schneier, B. (2015). *Data and Goliath: The Hidden Battles to Collect Your Data and Control Your World*, New York: W.W. Norton & Company.

be used for good, innocuous, or malicious disclosure (type 1 invasion), or for manipulation (type 3 invasion)? Consider geo-target marketing: marketing based on location data. A smartphone can register the frequency of a person's visits to a Catholic church. This data can subsequently be used in a political campaign or by calling upon voters to vote because catholic churchgoers in certain regions may be receptive to particular political messages or candidates.[7] Many users will not suspect that their church visits can be used to approach them in a political campaign.

Uncertainty about the importance of data. When there is uncertainty about the future meaning and use of data, users also do not know the possible significance of each of the data dots. For example, suppose that the finished mosaic generates a violation of privacy; some stones are widely available, while others are unique. Some stones are crucial in terms of perfecting the mosaic, while others are obsolete. A user does not know whether data is essential and rare, or of no consequence and abundantly available.

Metaphors offer insights, but they can also be misleading—and here a warning is appropriate. The mosaic metaphor suggests that many stones (data) are needed to produce information. This is not necessarily so, as data analysts may already come to far-reaching conclusions about someone's profile based on limited data. The essence of the Cambridge Analytica scandal exemplifies this (see Chapter 1, Section 4), as users can be profiled with a fairly limited dataset.

Disclosures versus reconstructions

Secondly, the photograph is, more or less, an objective representation of reality. Of course, a photo can subsequently be framed and

---

7   Eaton, J., (2019). *Catholics in Iowa went to church. Steve Bannon tracked their phones*, ThinkProgress, https://archive.thinkprogress.org/exclusive-steve-bannon-geofencing-data-collection-catholic-church-4aaeacd5c182/.

accompanied by interpretations and comments, which may be dubious, but there is always an approximately objective source. The world of data is different. Connecting data dots can result in a certain meaning, which is only limitedly based on, or entirely removed from, reality. There is a well-known proverb: 'if you torture the data long enough, it will confess'—and this also applies here. Malicious persons can play with data dots and construct malicious images.

This may be related, in a risky way to type 1 violations, disclosures. The data is tortured to the point that a certain meaning is construed that is damaging to the victim. In such a situation, the privacy violation is not a disclosure of a reality that should have remained private, but the construction of a fake reality that may be just as harmful. An incorrect representation of reality may also be dangerous in terms of type 2–4 privacy violations—profiling and manipulating. I have already addressed this in Chapter 1; people have an ambiguous, multi-layered identity, and this identity may be frozen by digital profiling and deviate significantly from their "real identity".

From useless to useful data

Thirdly, while data may be useless and reside at the bottom of the Internet ocean today, tomorrow the same data may be quite valuable. New technologies or new services can give more value to existing health data. Companies that are conscious of this useless–useful mechanism will have a strong impetus for the gathering of data. The more data available, the bigger the chance will be that the dataset will contain data that may suddenly increase significantly in value.

2.4 The spaghetti-like network of data-producing devices

The camera and the tabloid are the vehicles for old-school privacy violations. I will briefly point out the modern-day vehicles and this is a much more complicated story.

Engagement data

Of course, the pre-Web camera used by old school paparazzi does not necessarily need to take pictures—taking a photo is a clear choice. Whoever uses a smartphone, or any other device connected to the Internet, generates engagement-data— data about contacts, and the place, time, and duration of use. In other words, devices cannot avoid gathering data, as a lot of data is the by-product of a device, and this might result in a privacy invasion. Take the emergence of virtual money—banknotes are no longer made of paper but are stored in a wallet on our smartphone. A virtual coin can play an essential role in the fight against money laundering or terrorism—and offers a central bank real-time insight into the nature and size of transactions and, as such, a better insight into the effects of, for instance, monetary stimulus measures.[8] Simultaneously, data is released of every individual, about what has been bought where at what price. These "by-products" of introducing a virtual coin are potentially a massive threat to citizens' privacy.

Multi-functional devices...

The camera has only one function: taking pictures. Many devices in the Internet world are a platform for an array of functions. The car is not only a driving object but also a device connected to the Internet—and car systems deal with the totality of life as they concern a person's driving behaviour, daily routes and routines, the state of the car, but also their music choices or favourite news channels. This data is interesting for insurers, marketeers, route-planner companies, governments, and, of course, car manufacturers, who can offer more safety and convenience with the help of data.[9]

8   Mukherjee, A. (May 23, 2020). *China's Crypto Is All About Tracing — and Power*, BloombergOpinion.
9   Bertoncello, M., Camplone, G., Mohr, D., Möller, T., Wee, D., Gao, P., and Kaas, H-W. (2016). *Monetizing car data: New service business opportunities to create new customer benefits*, McKinsey & Company.

An interesting detail here is that police officers who want to search a particular property require a search warrant to do so, but a car can be searched at will. However, what is the difference between searching a house and a car when currently a car is the location of so much personal information? Should, perhaps, a counterpart of the search warrant be developed for searching vehicle data?[10]

...embedded in arcane networks

Devices are embedded in a complex device network, a network with a spaghetti-like structure. A smartphone has a vast number of apps, which can exchange data, and which are embedded in social networks that receive a flow of data. Many other devices are connected to the Internet, including cars, washing machines, and security cameras. The devices are interconnected in a way that is nearly impossible to unravel. The apps communicate mutually on the smartphone; the smartphone is connected to the car, which is, from time to time, connected to open Wi-Fi, and so there are many ways by which data leakage can happen.

Furthermore, the more devices and functions that are connected to the Internet, the more spaghetti there will be; the more spaghetti, the more demand will occur for all-in-one services, which may organize some form of order in the chaos. One may think of Intelligent Personal Assistants (e.g., Amazon's virtual assistant Alexa), who take on managing home devices and thus can absorb a vast amount of data.[11] Or think of the Chinese We-Chat, with which users cannot only send messages and imagery but can also make payments, buy goods and services, and read

10   Barrett, L. (2017). Herbie Fully Downloaded: Data-Driven Vehicles and the Automobile Exception. *Georgetown Law Journal*, *106*, pp. 181–208.

11   Bolton, T., Dargahi, T., Belguith, S., Al-Rakham, M. S., and Sodhro, A. H. (2021). On the Security and Privacy Challenges of Virtual Assistants. *Sensors*, *21*(7), p. 2312, doi: 10.3390/s21072312.; Furey, E., and Blue, J. (2019). *Can I Trust Her? Intelligent Personal Assistants and GDPR, International Symposium on Networks, Computers and Communications* (ISNCC), pp. 1–6.

the news. More functions mean more data and more meta-data and, as such, a continuously refined image of the user. Through function accumulation WeChat is a vital tool in the hands of the Chinese surveillance state.[12]

2.5 The villain comes in many guises

There are two villains in our story about the photograph: the photographer and the tabloid's editor. Both villains fit within a right–wrong scheme. First, it is wrong to take a person's picture that concerns a personal situation and to sell this photograph to a tabloid. Second, it is wrong to publish this photograph in a tabloid.

Delineating the villain in the Internet world is less straightforward, and the same is true of the victim. So, what do villains look like?

The benevolent villain

The ambiguous character of the villain is nowhere as clear if we consider the case of Facebook. With its ambition of 'connecting people', Facebook offers free services, which are greatly appreciated by its users. But, simultaneously, Facebook harvests data on a grand scale, and currently and regularly plays a role in privacy scandals. Indeed, several perceptions exist of Facebook:

- Facebook as the philanthropist—which considers its users as beneficiaries. Thanks to Facebook, users can share their experiences and knowledge at no cost and the world improves as a result, becoming more open and connected.
- Facebook as a highly valued service provider—which considers its users as paying clients. However, they do not pay with money but with their data and the time they spend on Facebook, which they are more than willing to give.

12 Chen, Y., Mao, Z., and Qiu, J. L. (2018). *Super-sticky WeChat and Chinese Society*, Bingley: Emerald Publishing.

- Facebook as the beneficiary—and its users are philanthropists. Users make their data available at no expense, which is a goldmine for Facebook.
- Facebook as a shady employer that owns a production factory. The users are the employees who offer their data and time as input, with Facebook being seen as an employer who does not pay its employees.
- Facebook as a coloniser who robs users of their data and occupies and exploits their private domains. The user is not Facebook's client, rather, the user is Favebook's product, which is made as attractive as possible to advertisers.
- Facebook as a feudal ruler. Users are wholly dependent on Facebook, and it is almost impossible to leave the platform. As such, users and their data have become captives of Facebook, without an exit option.

Not only does a host of different images exist—from philanthropist to colonizer to feudal ruler—but these images may also coincide. In case of a breach of privacy, this may be the work of a malicious villain, who hacks data and uses it to blackmail people. But the many faces of Facebook also show that the villain can have a friendly look, and this is equally true for other providers. The villain might be Janus-faced—it is a benevolent villain.

The unfortunate or careless villain

There are two interesting distinctions in the literature on law enforcement that are also applicable to privacy issues: (a) benevolent and malevolent actors and (b) competent versus incompetent actors.[13] Combining these two dimensions results in the figure below.

13 Baldwin, R., and Cave, M. (1990). *Understanding Regulation: Theory, Strategy and Practice*, Oxford: Oxford University Press, pp. 101–102.; Kagan, R. A., and Scholtz, J. T. (1984). The Criminology of the Corporation and regulatory Enforcement Strategies. In K. Hawkins and J. M. Thomas (Eds.), *Enforcing Regulation*, Boston: Kluwer-Nijhoff Publishing.; Kagan, R. A., and Scholtz, J. T. (1984). The Criminology

	Competent	Incompetent
Benevolent	I	II Unfortunate villain
Malevolent	III Malicious villain	IV Careless villain

figure 2.3 Three types of villains

Obviously, there is no villain in quadrant I of Figure 2.3 (benevolent and competent), but the remaining quadrants provide three different types of villains.

There are malicious villains (competent and malevolent). One can think of governments who are highly competent and possess the technology to gather and abuse data, and who intentionally and illegally spy on their citizens.

There is the unfortunate villain, who is benevolent but not sufficiently competent. Hospitals may sometimes be heavily fined on less-than-careful handling of patient data. Often no harm is intended in this case but there is still an element of incompetence. This does not alter the fact that there remains a villain in this case; incompetence can be culpable, and hospitals should have their competencies up to par. But, from the perspective of governance, it matters whether a villain is malicious or unfortunate.

And then there is the case of the careless villain. This villain who has no interest whatsoever in the value of privacy and is, as such, malevolent. Simultaneously, the careless villain lacks the competencies to protect privacy and does not invest in its development. The unfortunate villain does value privacy and thus has an intrinsic incentive to invest in competencies—the careless villain effectively lacks this incentive.

In law enforcement literature, the malicious villain often requires a penal approach from the government, while the

of the Corporation and regulatory Enforcement Strategies. In K. Hawkins and J. M. Thomas (Eds.), *Enforcing Regulation*, Boston: Kluwer-Nijhoff Publishing. (pp. 111–113).

unfortunate villain needs a more educational approach. The careless villain is situated somewhere in between these two cases.

The many hands

The violation of privacy is a process, which, in addition, is not entirely predictable: we do not know now whether the current collection of data will lead to a subsequent privacy violation. Moreover, in this process the problem of "many hands" often occurs. There are companies who gather and sell, other companies that analyse this data, and still others that use this data to improve their services. The normative question is who, in this chain of events, is ultimately responsible for the privacy violation? The empirical question then becomes: Which actors have the most impact on the ultimate privacy breach, so that governance can focus on these actors?

Today's villain is tomorrow's hero, and vice versa

Gathering data is part of many companies' business and innovation models: companies profit from the gathering of data and data harvesting defines their innovation potential. Innovations in the world of data are highly emergent. For those who are not familiar with the terminology: innovations can be planned and can emerge.
- A planned innovation is goal oriented. First, there is an idea about a new product or service, and subsequently it is determined what data is needed.
- An emergent innovation is the opposite: through the continuous accumulation of data, new and sometimes unforeseen possibilities for new products and services appear.

This emergent character of innovation provides a strong incentive for companies to get their hands on as much data as possible: more data means more innovation potential. Moreover, data currently without any significant meaning may turn out to have a lot of meaning tomorrow because, for instance, new technologies or new analytical tools may become available.[14] Two examples of emergent innovations:

- Small devices attached to undergarments enable the continuous gathering of data about a person's physical condition. This data offers advantages that can hardly be predicted, be they for medical research, monitoring a person's health, determining the trajectory of epidemics, et cetera. When so many potential innovations exist, there may be a strong impetus to gather this data. Innovation is an emergent process: first, collect data, then learn how to make that data beneficial.

- With the steep rise of online education, more and more data is being gathered on students—on the amount of time studied per learning unit, on what they do and do not understand, on questions being correctly or incorrectly made, and on the type of student who has enrolled in the course. For most data, it is not ex-ante clear what its meaning is and how it may contribute to the improvement of education, so there may also be an impetus to gather as much data as possible.

The collection of vast amounts of data today may lead to a new form of service tomorrow, which maybe highly appreciated by users or society. This means that today's villain, who is harvesting excessive volumes of data, may be tomorrow's hero. Of course, it might also be the other way around: today's hero, who offers a highly appreciated service, may be tomorrow's villain if it becomes clear that the service comes with many privacy invasions.

2.6 Distribution cannot be distinguished from production

The distribution of the photograph discussed above has two distinct features.

---

14   Schneier, B. (2015). *Data and Goliath: The Hidden Battles to Collect Your Data and Control Your World*, New York: W.W. Norton & Company. (p. 42).

The first feature is that the distribution is a sequential and linear process. The photograph is published in the tabloid, after which the tabloids are printed and subsequently transported to the readers through a distribution network—they move from A to B.

The second feature is the clear distinction that can be made between the object of the privacy violation (the photograph in the tabloid) and its distribution (the journey from the printing company to the reader).

The spaghetti metaphor that I introduced above, is also relevant for the distribution process. All kinds of devices are connected to the Internet; the devices are interconnected, and different users pair different devices. What does this spaghetti-like structure signify in terms of the distribution of the privacy violation? The most important concepts have been addressed in the previous sections, but I will point these out again shortly.

Production and distribution are parallel processes

In the spaghetti structure, data and privacy-sensitive information are shared everywhere, and there are ample opportunities for third parties who want to harvest this information and data. Whether this involves a vulnerable, open Wi-Fi connection or Facebook's tracking pixels, information and data can be continuously tapped. Therefore, there is no sequential process of creating an object (the picture) and distributing the object, instead, these are continuous parallel processes.

Production and distribution are emergent, unpredictable processes

Users relinquish data to parties who offer services—from Google to car manufacturers, from Airbnb to the hospital. This data may converge at any given time and place; the data dots are connected and enable the occurrence of a privacy violation. These connections happen because consumers consent to pairing various apps, or simply because certain companies harvest data from entirely different sources. This means that privacy invasion is not a linear process (from collecting a dataset to the invasion) but rather an emergent, capricious process. The privacy violation emerges in the spaghetti-like network.

Networks both distribute and create the privacy invasion

The ultimate object of privacy violation happens within the network where the data is being distributed. As such, the differentiation between the object of the privacy violation and its distribution becomes obscure. In the pre-Web world, the privacy violation is first produced (the photograph, the tabloid) before it is distributed. However, in our data-driven world, the network not only distributes the privacy violation—it also creates it.

2.7   The addressee as victim and villain

In the pre-Web world, the chain of privacy violation ends with the addressee, the person who sees the photograph in the tabloid. The victim and the villain in the world of data are ambivalent actors, and the addressee also plays an ambivalent role. The addressee is both villain and victim.

The addressee as the villain

The attention addressees show for information constituting privacy invasions, makes this information more valuable. More attention often means more revenue (e.g., for the platform and for the provider of the information), and may imply that amplification algorithms lead other users to this information. Thus, privacy violation is a circular process: privacy is invaded, the addressee consumes the invasion and bolsters the privacy violation.

Now, of course, the attention of one individual attendee is of limited significance, but the collective attention of all individuals causes the privacy violation to be amplified. There is a parallel with drug use. Hard drugs are illegal and are associated with very violent crime. Those who swallow an MDMA pill perpetuate the hard-drug trade and, therefore, violent crime. The effect of an individual consumer on drugs-related crime is very low, but the impact of all individuals together is very high. Individual users of MDMA pills are therefore sometimes addressed with moral arguments: everyone who takes a pill contributes to violent crime. A similar process applies to paying attention to privacy violations, as attention contributes to invasions of privacy.

The addressee as the victim

Whoever shows an interest in other people's data and information, relinquishes their own data in turn, which may be used for profiling or influencing. To a certain extent, this makes the user a co-victim. Suppose person A is the victim of a privacy violation, for example, highly personal health information has been posted on the Internet. Person B, the addressee, is interested in this particular information. A third party can probably gather data about this interest. It will become clear that B is interested in person A and/or this particular health issue. Again, privacy violation is a circular process, not a linear one. A linear process implies that (1) there is a privacy invasion of a victim, (2) one that is caused by a villain, and (3) from which an addressee will benefit. Circularity means that the addressee can, in turn, become the co-victim and the co-villain.

Consider the following thought experiment. Imagine a person being the victim of a privacy violation type 1, where personal pictures of this person have been posted on the Internet. Suppose this person perceives the cost of this violation as very low. There is exposure, but this is not a big issue for the victim. Let us presume that particular addressees, who show a more than average interest in the exposure, relinquish crucial data of themselves and their interest in the pictures. The data is then combined with other data, and it turns out that these addressees are very much interested in person A. The following question can then be posed: Who is more of a victim of the privacy violation, the original victim, who perceives the cost of the exposure as low, or the addressees, who clearly have an obsessive interest in person A?

2.8 The essence of the differences between then and now

Figure 2.4 below presents a summary of the analysis in the previous sections. Let me first admit that pre-Web privacy is a more nuanced phenomenon than it is according to the outline presented in Figure 2.4.. The current victim is ambivalent, and a victim in the pre-Web world could be ambivalent, too. One may think of a celebrity who was, on the one hand, the victim of a privacy violation, but on the other, could experience considerable interest in the public attention that is inherent to the publishing of private photographs. I am not particularly interested in making the perfect comparison between then and now, but the comparison with the past serves as a heuristic method to determine the essence of present-day privacy violations.

A second remark can also be made of Figure 2.4. In the world of data and privacy, there are also privacy violations that meet the description of the 'from' column. This pertains, in particular, to the type 1 violation from Chapter 1, where personal information is published on the Internet (remember the example of revenge porn). This example is, of course, in no way ambiguous—it is morally wrong. Therefore, this is not a binary "from–to" overview. Many phenomena in the "from" column still exist, and new phenomena are added to these—to the 'to also' column.

Figure 2.4 shows the enormous complexity of the governance challenge, as nothing is what it seems to be. Governance is about tools and strategies that governments can use to protect their citizens' privacy. These tools and strategies should be able to handle the complexity of the governance challenge. Figure 2.4 now lists nearly 20 factors that define the complexity of privacy governance. This is not very functional for building a narrative about governance so, in this chapter's final section, I will reduce these factors to four key concepts.

	From	To also
Victim	Unambiguous - incentive to protect privacy, because …	Ambiguous - victim is sometimes at fault of the privacy violation, has a strong incentive to relinquish data
	… cost of privacy violation is high, benefits are limited	Benefits now, costs later Benefits certain, costs uncertain Benefits for the individual, costs for the collective
	Unambiguous normative scheme	Normative scheme is ambiguous
Object	Information	Data, future use and meaning may be uncertain
	Information violates privacy	Data also has a (potentially) positive function
	The information is more or less an objective representation of reality	Collecting the dots may result in an 'incorrect' representation of reality
	Limited innovation	Many innovations. Innovation can suddenly make hitherto useless data, useful - so strong incentives for gathering data
Device	Relinquishing information/data is not necessary	Relinquishing data is a sine qua non for whoever goes online; often a by-product of other features of the device
	The device is mono-functional	The device is multi-functional, so there is an accumulation of functions and therefor of data
	The device is a stand-alone device	The device is connected to and embedded in the network of devices, incentive for development of all-in-one services
Villain	The villain is a clear villain	The villain is much more ambivalent or even benevolent
	The villain is wrong	There is a variety of villains – from malicious to careless and unfortunate
	The villain is traceable	The privacy violation is caused by 'many hands'
	Once a villain, always a villain	Today's villain, may be tomorrow's hero – because of emergent innovations
Distribution	Sequential process	Continuous parallel processes
	Linear process	Emergent, partly unpredictable process
	Distinction object and distribution of the object	Distinction object and distribution quite vague or non-existent
Addressee	Is consumer of the privacy violation	Is co-victim and co-villain
	The trajectory from victim to addressee is a linear process	The trajectory from victim to addressee is a circular process

figure 2.4 *Comparisons of privacy violation in the pre-Web world and presently*

governance. This is not very ... for fulfilling to narrative

2.9 The complexity of the governance challenge, summarized

Ambiguity, including split incentives, no uniformity

Privacy violations originate in data sharing, but data sharing is permanently embedded in a trade-off. Relinquishing data facilitates a service (health care, comfort, helpful information) that is of value—sometimes great value—to a user. Thus, the governance of privacy is the governance of competing values: privacy versus other values. When a government heavily focuses on privacy violations in medical care, this may deteriorate these competing values. This makes governance an ambiguous challenge, one that entails ambivalent victims, villains, and addressees. Interventions supporting privacy may result in something good becoming lost—e.g. in poorer care, less good search results, less innovative teaching.

An essential aspect of this ambiguity is the fact that users are often faced with "split incentives". The revenue of relinquishing the data is clear and immediately visible. However, the cost of relinquishing data is often diffuse—it will come later, or not at all, or apparently not at all. "Split incentives" are weak incentives for being careful with one's data.

Emergence and uncertainty, no planning, and certainties

There are many hands in complex, spaghetti-like networks in which an object and a distribution process cannot be distinguished. Within the complex and cluttered network of devices, there are incentives everywhere regarding sharing data and usage. Consequently, it is hard to ascertain where in this network the privacy violation lurks. Due to the many uncertainties, privacy violation is an emergent phenomenon and it might be challenging to predict where and when the breach will emerge. The metaphor here is that of the labyrinth—in certain places, things can go wrong, but one needs to continuously look for where this might be the case.

Dynamics, no stability

In the preceding analysis, almost every variable comes with dynamics. New services are introduced, and thus new trade-offs between the relinquishing of data and services must be made. Therefore, new incentives for data sharing occur so that the villain becomes less ambiguous, or the already-capricious process of distribution changes course. It is not just new services that result in this dynamic, there are also new technologies, new regulations, changing opinions on the value of privacy, and competing values. Dynamics are, of course, of great consequence for governance, meaning that every intervention of today runs the risk of becoming obsolete tomorrow.

Variety, no uniformity

All this ambiguity presents itself in an infinite number of different situations. Every individual can weigh the cost and revenue of the relinquishing of data in a different way. Every service may require a separate weighing of the costs and benefits of data sharing. Each societal context may lead to other deliberations. The more uniform the object of governance, the simpler that governance will be; the more variety the object has, the more complex the governance will be.

Again, there are also privacy invasions that are not characterized by this complexity—companies that do not properly protect the data entrusted to them, revenge porn, and unauthorized access to patient files. In each of these cases, there is an un-ambiguous violation of privacy, there are no uncertainties, and variety and dynamics do not matter (revenge porn is always wrong, for example). In many other situations, however, privacy is a much more ambiguous concept, and these characteristics do matter.

But enough about the complexity of the challenges—on to the approach governments may choose in coping with these challenges.

3   An Introduction to Governance

3.1   Introduction

Here is the argument thus far: privacy is a process and a layered concept (Chapter 1) and the tools and strategies that governments use must be able to cope with the complexity of privacy protection (Chapter 2). In this chapter I present various general governance concepts, which will be further outlined in the following chapters.

3.2   State, market, and society

The literature on governance distinguishes between state-, market-, and society-led approaches to governance.[1] The idea is that change (e.g., a better protection of privacy) can be realized by using the power of states, through market-mechanisms, and through activating people and communities. A government that seeks to improve the quality of public transportation can regulate quality (state), can promote quality by allowing more competition between transportation companies (market), and can promote quality by increasing the power and influence of travellers' organizations (society). There is a closely related distinction between hierarchy, markets, and networks[2]—a government may use its hierarchical power, use market mechanisms, or activate societal networks.

---

1   See, for example: van Vliet, M., and Dubbink, W. (2018). Evaluating Governance: State, Market and Participation Compared. In J. Kooiman et al. (Eds.), *Creative Governance*, London: Routledge, doi: org/10.4324/9780429463761.
2   Powell, W. (1990). Neither market nor hierarchy: Network forms of organization. In L. L. Cummings, and B. M. Staw (Eds.), *Research in Organizational Behavior*, Greenwich: JAI Press, pp. 295–366.

Legal, economic, and communicative instruments

Interventions using the power of the state, the market, or society, require the deployment of policy instruments or tools. In the literature, a host of typologies of policy instruments is presented. There is a well-known distinction between three kinds of "instrument-families" that together create a government's toolkit: its legal, economic, and communicative instruments.[3] Each of these instrument-families can limit or expand the behavioural options of the target groups.[4]

– Legal instruments. Behavioural options can be limited by prohibiting the use of soft drugs or closing a street to traffic. Behavioural options can be expanded by granting certain rights, such as the right to strike, the right to own weapons, and the right to assemble and associate.

– Economic instruments. Levies or user charges are economic instruments that limit behavioural options. Particular behaviours come with costs, making these behaviours a less attractive option—at least, that is the assumption. There also are economic instruments that expand options, such as subsidies or grants.

– Communicative instruments. An anti-smoking campaign is a communicative instrument aimed at limiting behavioural options. It encourages people not to smoke. A campaign can also be focused on increasing knowledge about a certain topic and to empower addressees. Here, we speak of communicative instruments that expand behavioural options.

3   de Bruijn, H., and ten Heuvelhof, E. (1998). A contextual approach to policy instruments. In B. G. Peters, and F. K. M. van Nispen (Eds.), *Public Policy Instruments. Evaluating the Tools of Public Administration*, Cheltenham: Edward Elgar. (pp. 11–32).; Howlett distinguishes authoritative, financial and information-based instruments: Howlett, M. (2010). *Designing public policies: Principles and instruments*, Abingdon: Routledge.

4   van der Doelen, F. C. J. (1998). The "Give-and-Take" Packaging of Policy Instruments: Optimizing Legitimacy and Effectiveness. In M-L. Bemelmans-Videc, R. C. Rist, and E. Vedung (Eds.), *Carrots, Sticks & Sermons*, New York: Routledge.

Often, in practice, a mix of these instruments will be deployed. Take the simple example of a speed limit—the law will dictate the maximum permissible speed (legal instrument), an offender can be fined if they break that limit (economic instrument), and a government can design a campaign to point out the safety risks of driving too fast (communicative instrument).

Figure 3.1 shows the variety of possible interventions.[5] Governments can use the three types of instruments to harness the power of the state, or that of the market, or that of society. There are several examples:

–   State. Governments can use the power of the state by deploying legal instruments (e.g., by imposing the principle of data-minimization), economic instruments (fines for violations of the principle), and communicative instruments (education on the importance of the principle).

–   Market. The power of the market can be used by deploying legal instruments, for example, regulation that enables the breaking up of big companies. If these companies abuse their market power by eliminating smaller players, competition laws can be used to restore competition. More competition activates the power of the market, and might result in less accumulation of data (see also Chapter 5). A government can use economic instruments that harness the power of the market. A tax on polluting products leads to these products having a higher price and, subsequently, can lead to less demand. A well-designed privacy communication campaign (communicative instruments) could stimulate companies to invest more in privacy enhancing technologies and to present themselves as a

5   Legal instruments have a special position since economic instruments and communicative instruments often need to be shaped in a legal manner. A subsidy is an economic instrument, yet it is required that it be embodied in rules. As such, we see legal instruments in two variants: as a (1) limiting or expanding intervention, or (2) as also necessary in order to provide a legal framework for other instruments.

	State	Market	Society
Legal instruments			
Financial instruments			
Communicative instruments			

figure 3.1 *Types of government interventions*

privacy-friendly competitor. Again, the power of the market is activated.

— Society. A government can provide legal or financial or communicative support to groups or organizations that work for the protection of privacy and thus use the power of society. The effect may be that tech giants are confronted with more societally countervailing powers.

Here too, in practice, we mainly see hybrid forms, as the scheme primarily provides conceptual clarity. In discussing the governance toolkit, I will use the distinction between state (Chapter 4), market (Chapter 5) and society (Chapter 6). In each chapter, I shall also indicate which variety of instruments a government may deploy.

There is a fourth family of instruments that may be used in the battle for privacy: technology. Continuously, privacy-preserving or privacy-enhancing technologies are being developed at all layers of the system—from the most basic infrastructure to, eventually, the data-based service provision.

However, this book mainly focuses on policy instruments. The assumption is that proper deployment of legislative, economic, and communicative instruments should create the conditions and incentives for the development of privacy-preserving technologies. When particular forms of data-sharing are prohibited (legislative instrument), this may be an incentive to invest in technical tools to protect from backdoor attacks or to invest in the pseudonymization of data or "secret sharing", thereby cutting up data in privacy-insensitive units. If violation of this prohibition is sanctioned with a high fine (economic instrument), this may strengthen these incentives to invest in technical tools.

In order to understand the three families of instruments better, attention is not only required for the characteristics of an instrument. Equally important are:
- the context in which the instruments are being applied, and
- the underlying values and norms.

3.3   The context and the inevitable unintended effects

The effectiveness of instruments is not only dependent on the characteristics of the instruments, but also on the context in which they are being applied. Take an environmental tax on plastic packaging that is aimed at reducing the use of plastics. The effectiveness of this tax depends on the characteristics of the instrument, such as the level of taxation. However, the effectiveness significantly depends on a multitude of contextual variables such as a companies' financial positions, on public support for taxing, on the price elasticity of demand, and on innovations of plastics, e.g. the development of biodegradable plastics.[6]

The more complex the context, the harder it is to predict the effectiveness of instruments and the bigger the chance that contextual factors exist that disturb this effectiveness. In other words, the more complex the context, the more unintended effects will occur.

In Chapter 2, I indicated that the context within which privacy has to be protected is extremely complex; it is defined by ambiguity, uncertainty, variety, and dynamics. In such a context, the effectiveness of instruments is difficult to predict and will go hand in hand with many unintended effects (see Figure 3.2).

6   de Bruijn, H. de, and ten Heuvelhof, E. (1998). A contextual approach to policy instruments. In B. G. Peters, and F. K. M. van Nispen (Eds.), *Public Policy Instruments. Evaluating the Tools of Public Administration*, Cheltenham: Edward Elgar, pp. 69–84.

	Intended effects	Unintended effects
Positive effects	I Protection of data, patient in charge	II More opportunities for scientific research
Negative effects	III More red tape	IV Less proper care

figure 3.2 *The various effects of instruments*

Figure 3.2 distinguishes between an instrument's positive and negative effects, and between intended and unintended effects. It displays a number of examples of these effects. Suppose that a regulatory instrument is designed that limits the possibilities of exchanging patients' personal data. Of course, a positive intended effect of this instrument is better protection of patient data and the patient having more control of their data (quadrant I).

Better data protection inevitably leads to more bureaucratic procedures and red tape. That is a negative but intended effect—an effect that is tolerated given the importance of privacy (quadrant III). Better protection of data-privacy may lead to poorer care. For example, it may make the peer-review of complex cases more complicated, which is a negative and unintended effect (quadrant IV). There are also unintended, positive effects. It is conceivable that privacy-regulation forces professionals to depersonalize cases and to encode data, and data encoding may result in new possibilities for scientific research (quadrant II).[7] Quadrant II clarifies that privacy should not be too easily contrasted with other values—privacy versus health, privacy versus economic growth, privacy versus innovation. The protection of data can also have a positive effect on these 'competing values'[8] such as, in this example, more opportunities for scientific research.

7   Ash, J. S., Berg, M., and Coiera E. (2004). Some unintended consequences of information technology in health care: the nature of patient care information system-related errors. *Journal of the American Medical Informatics Association*, 11(2), pp. 104–112.
8   Acquisti, A., Curtis T., and Wagman, L. (2016). The Economics of Privacy. *Journal of Economic Literature*, 54(2), pp. 442–492.

What does this imply for governance?

– The more complex a particular context, the greater the chance it will result in quadrant II, quadrant III, and quadrant IV effects. As made clear in Chapter 2, privacy governance has a complex context and so these effects will occur often.
– When an intervention is being undertaken, it is important to prevent negative effects to the highest possible extent and to harness the opportunities result from unintended positive effects.
– This strengthens the dynamics of privacy-governance. Instruments are designed and deployed and there are effects, amongst which are those of quadrants II, III and IV. A government may learn from this and adjust a toolkit or use additional tools.
– As such, governance is a process whereby instruments are developed and applied and intended and unintended effects provide lessons-learned, after which instruments may be adjusted accordingly.

3.4   The dynamics of underlying norms

Instruments are based on or rooted in values and norms. A norm indicates what is desired and good behaviour. Norms originate from values—a value is an ideal. For example, safety is a value that can be translated into a norm; because of safety, a government may establish a maximum speed on the highway. In turn, this has to be translated into a toolbox that includes:
– legislation, in which the maximum speed is defined (legal instruments),
– a system of traffic fines (economic instruments), and
– information about the dangers of driving too fast (communicative instruments).

Instruments pertain to the how-question, norms to the what-question, and values to the why-question. When the norm—which, in the example above, is a maximum speed—has insufficient societal support, the legitimacy of instruments may be jeopardized.

Often, values are stable. This is partially because they are described at a high level of abstraction. The value of privacy itself is not in question and has been codified in the Universal Declaration of Human Rights:

'No one shall be subjected to arbitrary interference with his privacy, family, home or correspondence, nor to attacks upon his honour and reputation.'[9]

This value can be translated into various norms, which are focused on protecting citizens' privacy and minimizing the collection of data.

In many cases the norm will be undisputed, but it will have become clear by now that this norm can also have a number of problematic traits in terms of governance.

- The norm is ambiguous because it is part of a trade-off. Opposite to the sharing of data we find another norm, such as the quality of health, freedom of expression, safety and security. The trade-off can vary from situation to situation and from individual to individual.
- It is also important that normative beliefs about privacy are dynamic, particularly because of fast technological developments. New technological developments may lead to new services, and new services lead to new normative beliefs about the trade-off between these services and privacy.
- The norm is being translated into instruments, which are applied in a complex context, and this may lead to a host of unintended effects (see above). These unintended effects may lead to the adjustment of instruments, but also to new opinions about underlying norms. When privacy-protection in a particular sector results in bureaucracy and hassle, this might irritate users and may lead to the norm of privacy being put into perspective.

9   Article 12 of the Universal Declaration of Human Rights

To clarify this let us consider a thought experiment about facial recognition.

Systems of facial recognition can greatly influence privacy. Suppose a government chooses the norm that using facial recognition has to be prevented to the highest extent, since it is at odds with the value of privacy. How will this impact the development of the valuation of facial recognition?

– Option 1. We often have difficulty accepting the fact that some violent crimes remain unsolved. Imagine the rate of solving violent crimes becomes much higher, on account of facial recognition (this is a thought experiment, I am aware that the role of these types of technologies is often overestimated). The technology proves to work reasonably well and, in particular, through a dragnet search in the national drivers' license files, is able to identify many perpetrators. This may mean that the societal tolerance for unsolved crimes drops significantly—the idea that someone is molested and that the perpetrator remains unpunished, becomes increasingly unacceptable. This change of opinion may greatly impact the preferred trade-off between privacy and a higher percentage of crimes solved, which may be at the detriment of privacy. Moreover, it may weaken the underlying norm that facial recognition has to be limited to the fullest extent.

– Option 2. It is also conceivable that, with facial recognition, pictures that are posted on the Internet can be scanned. Those who are accidental passers-by in photos may be recognized in the future. Facial recognition can contribute significantly to the feeling that public-space anonymity is disappearing. This may mean that, in the future, we perhaps feel that it is less and less acceptable that someone takes photos in public places: on the beach, in the shopping street, at tourist attractions—places where there will always be passers-by. Maybe there will be more opposition to the haphazard posting of group photos on social media et cetera. In option 2, there will be support for the norm that facial recognition has to be limited as much as possible, and a different norm will arise, namely restraint in taking pictures and shooting videos in the public space. This norm could, over time, lead to new instruments, for example, local prohibitions to take pictures or shoot videos.

Here too we see that governance is a process. When public opinion shifts towards greater support for privacy protection, more support occurs for interventions on behalf of privacy. The opposite is also true: public opinion may shift at the detriment of privacy protection, and this may result in less legitimacy for government interventions.

3.5 When to use instruments: upstream or downstream?

The next question concerns when instruments are to be deployed. Before answering this question, I want to revisit the observation made in Chapter 1, namely, that privacy invasion is a process:[10]

- With a type 1 privacy breach, which is most similar to the traditional privacy violation, I used the metaphor of the earthquake and aftershocks and the metaphor of the dormant volcano. Both metaphors make it clear that privacy breaches are not a one-time activity but a continuous process. Privacy breaches can continually receive renewed attention (the aftershocks), or disclosed information may be innocuous today but may be a privacy breach tomorrow (the dormant volcano).
- In type 2, 3, and 4 privacy violations, data goes through processes resulting in profiling or manipulation and

10   We also see these notions with Solove, who summarizes the process in four steps: information collection, information processing, information dissemination and invasion. Solove, D. J. (2006). A Taxonomy of Privacy. *University of Pennsylvania Law Review, 154,* pp. 477–560.

intimidation—the data-journey or data stream. These processes go on continuously, and the entirety of these processes has a spaghetti-like structure. Every strand is a data-stream, the strands are non-linear, and the strands are often entangled. Often, it is not clear at the start of the data-stream or data-journey how data will be used, nor is it clear whether data-use will lead to a privacy violation.

- Privacy as a process has an important normative implication. During the data-journey, normative beliefs about data-use may vary. The initial perception may be that there is a privacy-issue (or not), but this perception may change during the data-journey. If normative views change, this can have major implications for privacy governance: the legitimacy of the deployment of tools can shift, and legitimacy is a *sine qua non* for the effective use of these instruments.

When privacy violation is a continuous process and when normative views can change during this process, the question emerges as to when, during the data-journey, instruments should be deployed? In an ideal–typical sense, there are two options:

- Ex ante, instruments to protect privacy need to be deployed as early as possible in the data-journey. This will limit the collection of data and thus prevent privacy breaches later during the journey. The data-journey may also be called a data-stream, and then we speak of the upstream use of instruments.
- Ex post, at the end of the data-journey. The focus should not be so much on data collection, but on data use. After all, it is only during the data-journey that it becomes clear what data is used for. In the language of the data-stream: interventions take place downstream or midstream.

These two lenses also lead to two different views as to what a privacy violation is. Through the ex-post lens, data-collection will only lead to a privacy violation, when it becomes clear how data is used. Through the ex-ante lens, data-privacy is a right, and data collection may be a privacy violation even when it is unclear what will happen with the data itself.[11]

Ex ante or upstream: prepare and prevent

Here, the idea is that privacy violations have to be prevented, and that the instruments of the three families should be deployed ex ante or upstream. This may, for example, relate to the process of designing a new service, whereby privacy should be taken into account as early and as much as possible. The analogy here is that of "building codes", the standards for constructing buildings. When these building codes are known ex ante, they will be of maximum influence on producers', contractors', and users' behaviour. Those who have proper building codes upstream are able to prevent a lot of trouble downstream, and can do so far ahead in the process. Moreover, they create stability and predictability, and so all parties involved know what is expected from them and from others.

What is the power of the ex-ante lens?
- When, early in the data-journey, there is attention to privacy, this will lead to less data-collection and so there will be less chance of privacy breaches occurring. The analogy of building codes is powerful here: ex ante established building codes have a positive impact on the subsequent construction processes.
- When there is a direct and immediate relation between data collection and privacy violation (the abuse of data does not occur once it is downstream, but already at the beginning of the data-journey), it is of course effective to intervene upstream. When users share sensitive data with a company and the company handles the data in a sloppy manner, we are, basically, at the beginning of the data-journey, but it may

11   See also Bygrave, L.A. (2017). Data protection by Design and by Default: Deciphering the EU's Legislative Requirements. *Oslo Law Review*, 4(2), pp. 105–120.; Yeh, C-L. (2018). Pursuing consumer empowerment in the age of big data: A comprehensive regulatory framework for data brokers. *Telecommunications Policy*, 42(4), pp. 282–292.

already be clear that privacy has been violated. In 2020, the Information Commissioner's Office (ICO) imposed a fine of £20 million on British Airways; users of BA's website were diverted to a fraudulent site, after which criminals succeeded in harvesting the data of 400,000 users, including their login data, credit card information, addresses, and itineraries. According to the ICO, the breach was the consequence of inadequate security arrangements. The ICO formulates the duty of care quite clearly: 'when you are entrusted with personal data, you must look after it'.[12]

- Downstream interventions may arrive too late, as the damage is already done and recovery from the damage is not entirely possible. An example is a patient file that contains too much information, and which has been viewed by unauthorized acquaintances of the patient. In such situations, prevention is better than curing.

- Ex ante governance is also relevant because it may prevent opportunistic behaviour. Imagine governance that solely comprises downstream interventions. A service provider who knows that there is the upstream opportunity for data-collection may optimize this opportunity: data is being harvested and a new service is being developed that will be introduced into the market. Subsequently, imagine that the service comes with a privacy invasion; when the use of the service increases in volume, an ex post intervention may be too late. The point of no return has already passed, and so an ex ante intervention might be more effective.

So, ex ante interventions may be effective but they are also subject to important limitations. I will show this with the aid of the concept "privacy by design".

12   Information Commissioner's Office (2020). ICO fines British Airways £20m for data breach affecting more than 400,000 customers. London ICO, October 22nd. https://ico.org.uk/about-the-ico/news-and-events/news-and-blogs/2020/10/ico-fines-british-airways-20m-for-data-breach-affecting-more-than-400-000-customers/

Example: privacy by design

"Privacy by design" is based on the principle of ex ante intervention: in developing new services, the value of privacy has to be considered as early as possible, even during the design process itself.

Norms one may think of include data minimization (only data necessary for the service is being requested), pseudonymization (personal data cannot be linked to a specific person), or storage limitation (as soon as the data-collection goal is been reached the person can no longer be identified). Privacy by design can be realized in the technical design of a service (storage-limitation, the automatic destruction of data). An analogy can be seen in a car blocking system whereby the engine cannot be started when the seatbelt is not fastened.[13] Privacy by design can also be realized by organizational or procedural measures, such as storage-limitation by organizational procedures that determine retention terms.

The principle of privacy by design appeals to common sense: take appropriate action upstream, to prevent problems downstream. However, privacy by design is also subject to major limitations.

First, concepts such as data-minimization and storage-limitation are ambiguous in many situations. They presuppose the existence of an uncontested and determined goal, against which can be measured whether data-collection is necessary and for how long it might be necessary. However, goals are not always clear, may change due to technological innovation, may be ambiguous, and are sometimes disputable. Ex ante interventions may generate high costs while there is no meaningful increase in privacy.[14]

13 Yeung, K. (2017). 'Hypernudge': Big Data as a mode of regulation by design. *Information, Communication & Society, 20*(1), pp. 118–136, doi: 10.1080/1369118X.2016.1186713.
14 See, for example, Doss, A. F. (2020). Cyber Privacy. *Who Has Your Data and Why Should You Care*, Dallas: BenBella Books.

Second, what does data-minimization mean when a service continuously innovates? Data that is not necessary today may be necessary tomorrow, after a service has been renewed. Data-minimization is related to a goal, but this goal may be moving. Think of algorithmic hyper-nudging; an individualized nudge is given, based on a continuous scan of data, that a human being can no longer process. Hyper-nudging problematizes the principle of data-minimization because the goal of data-collection can gradually and continually shift.

Third, privacy by design entails the thought that the development of new services is a more or less linear process, reminiscent of the traditional waterfall-planning. This is not the case, particularly in the innovative world of data and privacy. There is no waterfall-planning, rather, there is agile development: functionalities are tested and renewed continuously in order for users to be able to receive continuous updates of these functionalities. Agile development heavily rests on the idea of modularity—a service is being modularized and added to other services, so there is no clear distinction between the initial development (upstream) and the usage thereafter (downstream).[15]

This all happens on a grand scale. The enormous variety of modules is continuously worked on and the modules themselves are continuously upgraded and, moreover, may interfere in many different manners. Regulating privacy aspects upstream? This may be very hard, there may be too many unknowns, too many dynamics, and too much variety.

Fourth, this reasoning assumes that we know upstream what the societal value of new technology will be, but this value is sometimes hard to predict. There is a well-known mechanism in the world of innovation: new technology often proves to be the solution to problems that were not yet recognized when the solution itself did not exist. This simple fact problematizes the idea

15   Gürses, S., and van Hoboken, J. (2017). In J. Polonetsky et al. (Eds.) *Privacy after the agile turn, Cambridge Handbook of Consumer Privacy.*Cambridge: Cambridge University Press.

Privacy by Design promising	Privacy by Design problematic
PbD has a unambiguous meaning	PbD has an ambiguous meaning
Goals of data-usage stable	Goals of data-use change
Development of technology and services is a more or less linear process	Development of technology and services is an agile, iterative process
Societal value of service is known and stable	Societal value unknown and may change

figure 3.3 *Privacy by Design - possibilities and limitations*

of privacy by design. The more innovation potential a service has, the more difficult it is to make an ex-ante trade-off between this service and privacy. In fact, when this trade-off is made early in the design process, it can hinder subsequent innovation processes.

These four objections do not imply that privacy by design is meaningless—rather, they show that it has its limitations, which are outlined in Figure 3.3 below.

Ex post or downstream: respond and restore

When ex ante interventions are problematic (the right-hand column of Figure 3.3), the alternative is an ex-post intervention. This may entail:
- when a privacy-violation looms, an intervention is done to prevent this, or,
- when a privacy-violation has taken place, its damage is repaired as soon as possible.

In the language of a data stream, the attention shifts from upstream interventions to midstream or downstream interventions—when the privacy-violation looms or has taken place. What is the power of this governance approach?
- It offers more possibilities for data-driven innovations. As mentioned above, data innovation potential is not always known upstream. Downstream intervention is also an acknowledgement for the fact that a process of

innovation does not run in a linear fashion. The result of an innovation process is known downstream, but in the upstream-phase, we do not know what course the data stream will take.

- The risk of ex ante governance is that the trade-off between privacy and other values is based on too little information. The earlier a government intervenes during the data-journey, the more uncertainties there are and the greater the chance of unintended effects. For instance, if a trade-off is being made between privacy and healthcare upstream, it will, by and large, be a binary issue—it concerns privacy versus care and, as such, an either–or situation as more care results in less privacy and vice versa. The later the weighing is being done, the more information will be available, and the more lessons can be drawn from this information as a result. The trade-off might prove to be much less binary than previously thought.

- Ex post governance offers space and can cope with changing political or societal preferences. When perceptions of public values change, data that today is considered a privacy invasion may tomorrow be crucial to the realization of important public values.

- When less data is being collected at the start of the data-journey, this does not automatically mean that there are less privacy-invasions at the end of the data-journey. Less personal data and more machine learning may also lead to privacy-invasion.[16] Moreover, legitimate data-gathering upstream can lead to privacy-violations downstream. In legislation, personal data is being protected, but non-personal data can sometimes be made personal.[17] This also

16   Morozov, E. (May 15, 2021). *Privacy activists are winning fights with tech giants. Why does victory feel hollow?*, The Guardian.
17   Narayanan, A., and Shmatikov, V. (2008). *Robust de-anonymization of large sparse datasets*, 2008 IEEE Symposium on Security and Privacy, pp. 111–125.; if data is anonymized, there is a residual risk that data can still be traced back to individuals: Michèle, F., and Pallas, F. (2020). They who must not be identified—distinguishing

requires governance ex post: the accent shifts from upstream protecting to downstream protecting against data-based inferences.[18]

Example: privacy versus innovation

Here is an example of the above in the form of a thought experiment. The value of privacy may require a trade-off with other values—in the following thought experiment, with innovation. Imagine the existence of two countries. Country A feels protection of privacy is an important value and develops a multitude of instruments to safeguard the privacy of its citizens based on the idea of ex ante governance. Country B highly values innovation, companies in country B see only limited hindrance in collecting data in order for as many innovations as possible to occur. Those who value privacy will prefer the policy of country A since, in country B, citizens have a lot less protection.

As country B has fewer restrictions, there are many more innovations in country B, including more safety in the streets, better healthcare, better and more tailored education. This can have important consequences:
–   Tolerance towards crime, suboptimal care, and poor education may decrease. A high level of safety, care, and education become the new normal and are beneficial to the quality of life.
–   Through the innovations, the trade-off between the value of privacy and the values of safety, proper care, and good education can change—in the current example, this comes at the cost of privacy.

personal from non-personal data under the GDPR. *International Data Privacy Law, 10*(1), pp. 11–36.
18   Wachter, S. and Mittelstadt, B. (2019). A Right to Reasonable Inferences: Re-Thinking Data Protection Law in the Age of Big Data and AI. *Columbia Business Law Review, 2019*(2), pp. 494–620, doi: 10.7916/cblr.v2019i2.3424.

Meanwhile, in country A, privacy is being properly protected but, as a result, there is less innovation within the police-force, within care, and within education. The question is then how long the strict privacy policy of country A will stand when citizens of A learn that public servicing in country B has a much higher standard. This may lead to changing opinions on the value of privacy and to a dramatic conclusion for country A. The normative views of privacy protection in country A shift in the direction of less privacy but, meanwhile, it significantly lags behind country B in a technological sense.

Furthermore, innovative companies in country A face more barriers than their competitors in country B; the risk is that country B will be much more attractive for innovative companies than country A. The innovations from country B will, in part, be used by citizens in country A. This results in a paradoxical outcome: country A, with its privacy protection, becomes dependent on country B in terms of data-driven services.

Now, let us also consider a country C which, just like country A, values privacy, but, just like country B, also wants to be innovative. This country may opt for allowing space for innovation and basing privacy governance on the strategy of ex post governance: there is a downstream intervention at the moment that privacy proves to be an issue.

- Sometimes, the innovation will lead to the diminishment of the value of privacy. For example, much better care will develop, and this will provide so much added value that privacy considerations should not stand in the way of this innovation. When there is societal consensus in regard to this new trade-off, this need not be a problem.
- Sometimes, this will not be the case, innovation will occur at the detriment of privacy and citizens or governments may feel that the importance of privacy outweighs that of innovation. This may lead to the adjustment or to the discontinuation of the innovation. Instead of protecting privacy ex ante (country A), a governance system can be built that offers space for innovation, but that also protects

privacy as soon as this innovation proves that it comes with too much privacy-violation.

Country C uses the middle-of-the-road approach: there is room for innovation, as long as companies stay alert to privacy.

There are also two important nuances here.

– As stated, the risk of ex post governance is its being too late. The service, including any related privacy-violation, has already passed the point of no return. The service is available and is already widely used, which makes downstream privacy protection very complicated.

– Ex ante interventions can be a disincentive to innovation, but this is not necessarily the case. Strict privacy regulations do not have to hinder innovation, they can also incentivize innovation or change its direction.[19] Ex ante governance might create a more predictable business environment than ex post governance. The disincentive for innovation is therefore a risk, not a foregone conclusion.

3.6   Resilient governance

What does this all mean for the governance of privacy?

In Chapter 1, the conclusion was that privacy and privacy violations are a process. A user shares data, which go through a process that may (or may not) lead to profiling or manipulation and, therefore, to privacy invasions (types 2–4). Alternatively, private information is made public, and and may subsequently prove harmful—the earthquake with the aftershocks, the dormant volcano becoming active (type 1).

Chapter 2 contains an analysis of the complexity of the governance challenge. The protection of privacy is a wicked issue because of the following four characteristics:

19   Goldfarb, A., and Tucker, C. (2012). Privacy and innovation. *Innovation Policy and the Economy*, *12*(1), pp. 65–90, doi: 10.1086/663156.

- Ambiguity: privacy almost always requires a trade-off with other values.
- Uncertainty: privacy issues manifest themselves during the data-journey and it is not always predictable when and in what form they will manifest themselves.
- Variety: there is a large number of different situations that require different trade-offs.
- Dynamics: new technologies and services are constantly emerging, which can lead to new trade-offs between privacy and other values.

In this chapter, a number of consequences of these characteristics have been identified:
- The effectiveness of government interventions is largely determined by these contextual characteristics.
- The more complex the context, the more often interventions will lead to unintended consequences.
- Interventions are embedded in normative beliefs about the relationship between privacy and other values, and these views may change over time.
- Upstream interventions—"prepare and prevent"—can be effective, but they also have important limitations due to the complexity of the context and the many uncertainties at the beginning of the journey, meaning that midstream and downstream interventions—"respond and restore"—are also necessary.

This all means that privacy protection requires "resilient governance".[20] Resilient governance is about learning and reflexivity, adaptation, and responsiveness. What does that mean?

---

20   Termeer, C. J. A. M., Dewulf, A., Breeman, G., and Stiller, S. J. (2015). Governance Capabilities for Dealing Wisely With Wicked Problems. *Administration & Society*, *47*(6), pp. 680–710.

Resilience (I): governance as a continuous process

The governance of privacy is not a one-off intervention, but a process of monitoring (how is data being used?), intervening (how and when can privacy be safeguarded?), learning (which data-use should be defined as privacy-violation and which data-use should be allowed; what are effective and ineffective interventions?), and adaptation (how should interventions, given lessons learned, be changed?) Privacy is a process, so the governance of privacy is also a process.

Resilience (II): governance as upstream, midstream, and downstream interventions

Resilient governance is a process of learning and adaptation, and this means also learning about the best moment to intervene. Sometimes a government can intervene upstream, sometimes this intervention is counter-productive, sometimes upstream interventions will have to be adjusted later. This means that not only upstream interventions, but also midstream and downstream interventions—"respond and restore"—are an important part of resilient governance. Resilient governance transcends the opposition between prepare/prevent and respond/restore.[21]

Resilience (III): governance as redundancy

There is resilient governance at the level of data-journeys, but there is also resilient governance at a systems level: the "whole" of data-journeys—the metaphor of the spaghetti-like structure. Nobody can oversee all data streams and there are many uncertainties, but the more incentives there are for privacy protection, the more likely it is that privacy breaches will be prevented. As

---

21   Rerup, C. (2001). "Houston, we have a problem": Anticipation and improvisation as sources of organizational resilience', *Comportamiento Organizacional e Gestao*, *7*(1), pp. 27–44.

such, resilient governance has a next meaning: resilience as redundancy. Redundancy means that there is a multitude of stimuli for a multitude of parties (government, market, and society) to be alert to privacy. The wicked nature of privacy violations means that it is not always clear which privacy violation will surface, or where and when it will surface. Redundancy makes a system less vulnerable; even when privacy violations are unforeseen, there might be incentives to prevent them or to restore privacy. Moreover, when some of the stimuli do not function well, the others may still offer sufficient protection.

Resilience (IV): governance as finding new trade-offs

Resilience can also relate to the trade-off between privacy and other values. In the process of monitoring, intervening, learning, and adapting, this trade-off can change. The existing balance between privacy and the other values shifts in favour of or against privacy based on new insights gained throughout the process itself. In the literature on resilience, this is an important notion: resilience can mean that the existing and disturbed balance between values is restored, but also that a new balance is found.[22]

In the following chapters, I will further elaborate on resilient governance from three perspectives. A government itself can intervene (Chapter 4), it can activate market mechanisms (Chapter 5), and it can invest in the empowerment of society (Chapter 6).

22 de Bruijne, M. L. C., Boin, A., and van Eeten, M. J. G. (2012). Resilience. Exploring the concept and its meaning. In L. K. Comfort, A. Boin, and C. C. Demchak (Eds.), *Designing Resilience. Preparing for Extreme Events*), Pittsburgh: University of Pittsburgh Press, pp. 13–32.

4   The Power of the State

4.1   Introduction

Which role can governments, with their regulatory toolboxes, play in the protection of privacy? I will answer this question by first focusing on the legal instruments of government. Financial and communicative instruments can be used by both private and public actors, but only governments can enact laws.

As stated in the previous chapter, privacy protection requires resilient governance. Governance (1) is a continuous process, (2) with upstream, midstream, and downstream interventions, (3) should result in redundant systems of incentives for privacy protection (or barriers for privacy invasions), and (4) may result in maintaining privacy, restoring privacy, or finding a new balance between privacy and other values.

This chapter will first present different types of regulation for resilience: goal-based regulation, procedural regulation, negotiated regulation, indirect regulation, and institutional regulation (Sections 2–6). In Section 7, I will explain how these types of regulation contribute to resilience. Section 8 contains a few concluding remarks about capacity and institution building.

4.2   From prescriptive- to goal-based regulation

The literature on regulation acknowledges a distinction between prescriptive regulation and goal-based—also referred to as performance-based—regulation.[1]

Consider the following simple example. A mayor is responsible for the peace and hygiene of a city's parks and wants to regulate

1   Coglianese, C., Nash, J., and Olmstead, T. (2003). Performance-based regulation: Prospects and limitations in health, safety, and environmental protection, *Administrative Law Review*, 55(4), pp. 705–729.

them accordingly. The mayor can give park managers the instruction to place signs stating "forbidden for dogs" in the parks, which would be a prescriptive regulation. The mayor imposes the means (the aforementioned signs) by which the goal of peace and hygiene is to be realized.

Goal-based or performance-based regulation means that the mayor imposes the objective, namely, to take care of peace and hygiene. The managers know what the end-state or the outcome has to be and have the liberty to determine by what means they will achieve this goal.[2]

There are several advantages to this approach. The managers are familiar with the local situation and will know how to strike the best balance between peace and hygiene on the one hand and other values on the other. In one neighbourhood, there may be a substantial need for open space for outdoor sports and exercise. In another area, there may be a greater need for space for families to relax or barbecue. The park manager can balance the values of peace and hygiene against these different local values.

Goal-based regulation and privacy

Let us move from city parks to the world of data and privacy. Privacy is an ambiguous concept because of the tension with one or more other values. Patients have a right to protection of their medical data, the right to "informational control". Opposite this, of course, we find the value of proper and professional care for the patient, and those values that pertain to collective health during, for example, a pandemic. Governance means that privacy has to be safeguarded, while those other values are also being considered.

In the current regulations, we find both prescriptive and goal-based rules. Information about someone's health is highly

2   Deighton-Smith, R. (2008). Process and performance-based regulation: challenges for regulatory governance and regulatory reform. In P. Carroll, R. Deighton-Smith, H. Silver, and C. Walker (Eds.), *Minding the Gap*, Canberra: University Printing Services.

personal, it is defined as 'special category data' under the European Union's GDPR and therefore has special protection.[3] Physicians who have access to this information can only share it after explicit consent has been granted by the 'data-subject' (the patient).

This condition of consent is an example of prescriptive regulation. However, there may be situations in which the trade-off between privacy and other values has to be made. The GDPR contains several articles that offer an opportunity for data usage, for example, when 'reasons of substantial public interest', or 'reasons of public interest in the area of public health'[4] are concerned—conditions that can be defined as goal-based regulation. The goal is that privacy is protected, while 'substantial public interests' or 'public interests in the area of public health' are taken into account.

The importance of such goal-based regulations became apparent during the Covid-19 pandemic, when the value of privacy had to be protected, but so too did the value of collective health. During the pandemic, the UK's NHS drew up a 'Shielded Patient List', a record of vulnerable patients.[5] Patient names were presented by general practitioners and hospitals based on the data they had access to. Patients on this list received public health messages by phone, text, or email, or could get quick consultations and diagnoses. Could this data be shared? Yes, says the UK regulator ICO, this was justified because of the 'substantial public interest' of the GDPR:[6]

'The ICO is a reasonable and pragmatic regulator, one that does not operate in isolation from matters of serious public concern.

---

3   Article 9, GDPR, Processing of special categories of personal data.
4   '[S]uch as protecting against serious cross-border threats to health or ensuring high standards of quality and safety of health care and of medicinal products or medical devices.' Article. 9.2 GDPR — both provisions have additional safeguards to protect privacy.
5   https://digital.nhs.uk/dashboards/shielded-patient-list-open-data-set.
6   House of Commons. (May 15, 2020). *Briefing Paper Patient health records: access, sharing and confidentiality.* https://commonslibrary.parliament.uk/research-briefings/sn07103/.

Regarding compliance with data protection, we will take into account the compelling public interest in the current health emergency.'[7]

The concrete example is less important here than the underlying mechanism, as the statement shows the power of goal-based regulation—it enables trade-offs, where prescriptive regulation does not. Prescriptive regulation limits the possibilities for data sharing upstream; goal-based regulation offers possibilities for making trade-offs midstream or downstream.

Everyone agrees that there should be space for goal-based regulation. Therefore, the discussion is not so much about the importance of goal-based regulation, but about the question under which conditions goal-based regulation may be used. Is goal-based regulation the fall back, one that can only be used under exceptional circumstances? Or should there be more space for goal-based regulation—is goal-based regulation the default? The answer to the latter question is, in part, political, and will depend on the weighing of values such as privacy and innovation, or opinions on the role of government.

Additionally, it is essential that space offered by goal-regulation will only be effective if it stimulates learning processes. To clarify this, I provide another example in the form of a thought experiment.

Imagine that a patient has given doctors permission to share health information from their patient files. Still, there may be situations in which one might doubt whether the sharing information of certain information will be covered by this consent. Suppose strict prescriptive regulation is used in the interest of privacy: when information is shared with physicians who are not covered by consent, separate consent must be given to those physicians. This will give the patient more informational control; the approach may work, but it might also fail. It may lead to a lot of bureaucratic hassle (the patient is continuously required to actively consent),

7   https://ico.org.uk/about-the-ico/news-and-events/news-and-blogs/2020/03/data-protection-and-coronavirus/.

to a less critical view on a treatment (new physicians aren't as readily invited to participate in peer consultations), to scheduling problems (a doctor who is suddenly unavailable cannot be replaced, and so a peer consultation should be postponed). The example shows the risk of prescriptive regulation as the emphasis lies so heavily on information control that professional care is at stake. Goal-based regulation may be a much more attractive option as the goal is that privacy is protected in light of proper and professional care, and this trade-off should be allowed to happen in the actual moment, either midstream or downstream.

However, the room for trade-offs provided by goal-based regulation can also be misused. In this thought experiment, perhaps the circle of involved medical professionals grows too big? Or perhaps far too much information is being shared? Goal-based regulation requires at least regular reflection from the professionals involved (in this case, the doctors), on these and other questions, and the formulation of answers to them. Goal-based regulation offers room and room requires reflection. These answers might develop into a shared vision of what proper practice is. In other words, the space that goal-regulation offers ideally leads to reflection, learning processes, and increased insight into what a good use of this space might be. Learning and reflection may result in best practices and, over time, even be codified in professional standards.

The design and implementation of these learning processes is a *sine qua non* for effective goal regulation. Without reflection and learning processes, there is always the risk of opportunism: the space of goal-based regulation is not used to make the best decision, rather it is misused to legitimize the sloppy handling of data and information.

What is the power of goal-based regulation and what are its limitations?

First. Goal-based regulation provides more space. The trade-off between privacy and other values is not made entirely upstream but is also made midstream or downstream. In the actual moment and in the concrete situation, there is space to weigh privacy and care, or privacy and innovation, or privacy and quality of service. Every situation is different, and different situations require other trade-offs—goal-based regulation facilitates this need for variety.

Second. Goal-based regulation can also lead to the empowerment of the regulatees; in the thought experiment about patient files, these would be the doctors. The regulatees have to weigh privacy against other values and take ownership for the final balance between privacy and care. If only the upstream, prescriptive regulation existed, this weighing would be outsourced to the regulator.

Third. Goal-based regulation may contribute to governance-as-a-learning-process. Medical professionals can learn under which conditions tension arises between privacy and good care, and the various ways of handling this—what works and what does not work, what are acceptable and what are unacceptable trade-offs?

Naturally, goal-regulation has its limitations too.

First, an important assumption is that regulatees using the possibilities of goal-regulation have good intentions, are sufficiently competent, and handle the space provided by goal-regulation in an appropriate fashion. The assumption will not always manifest in reality: regulatees might be reactive, sloppy, or even malicious.

Second, the further assumption is that regulatees will reach a consensus about the balance between privacy and other values. This will not always be the case—sometimes, regulatees will fundamentally disagree about the trade-off between privacy and other values, and disagreement can result in situations that are too unpredictable or obscure. In such cases, prescriptive regulation can be more efficient and can prevent all kinds of transaction costs.

Third. The next assumption is that regulatees have the competencies needed and—perhaps more importantly—dare to use the space offered by goal-regulation. After all, the trade-off between privacy and other values also implies risks: regulatees can make incorrect judgements with far-reaching consequences. Simply conforming to prescriptive regulation might be more attractive for risk-averse regulatees.

4.3 From substantive regulation to procedural regulation

The distinction between substantive regulation and procedural regulation can be clarified with the game-theoretical example of envy-free cake-cutting.

Two people want to share a cake. They both want a big piece and have clear preferences for the toppings and fillings. The result must be fair and acceptable to both parties—that is, "envy-free"—and a third person is to regulate the cake-cutting.

This third party disposes of two strategies. The first one is substantive regulation, which requires detailed rules about the size of the cake, the different kinds of toppings and fillings, and a set of criteria to determine the rights of the parties concerned. Substantive regulation entails the risk of ever-increasing complex rules being necessary to bring about a fair division. The second strategy is procedural regulation, which implies this third party merely prescribes a procedure.

This procedure may entail the two parties getting different roles:

- the first party cuts the cake and can decide what the size of the two pieces will be;
- the second party gets to be the first to choose.

What is going on here? This procedure contains strong incentives for a fair distribution of the cake. People who can choose first, choose the best piece for themselves. The person who can cut knows this and therefore has a strong incentive to cut two equal pieces, which will increase the likelihood of an envy-free solution.

For third parties, the advantage of procedural regulation is that they do not become entangled in a set of detailed and content-based rules, which require ever-increasing refinement to lead to a good outcome. A simple procedural rule suffices. The more complex the regulation of a particular issue is, the more attractive procedural regulation may be.

Procedural regulation and privacy

From cake-cutting to privacy. Companies can be confronted with data breaches, with the consequence of severe privacy violations for their clients. Here, we see a tremendous variety of situations: different kinds of data, different types of breaches, and different types of effects on different types of clients. A regulator who wants to prescribe the handling of violations, and who mainly approaches the issues in a substantive manner, has at least one of the following two problems:

– It may require precise and detailed regulation since too many different situations have to be dealt with, something that can result in the risk of over-regulation and bureaucracy.
– The risk of under-regulation: the regulation is too generic and provides too little direction for the regulatees. This is not only a problem for the regulator but also for the regulatees themselves, who might be faced with much uncertainty regarding the enforcement of the rules.

The alternative is regulation that requires organizations to report data breaches to the regulator and to their clients.[8] This data breach notification legislation is predominantly procedural: it prescribes the procedure to be followed in case of a data breach. The underlying thought here is that this procedure is a stimulus for companies to invest in data security. A company that has to report a breach may suffer significant reputational damage. Clients who are informed of data breaches may opt for another service provider, or for better protecting for their data.[9]

A second example: procedural rules may play a role in selling data. Howard uses the arms sales metaphor. Arms manufacturers can be obligated to inform a government agency as to which

8   Bisogni, F. (2020). *Information Availability and Data Breaches. Data Breach Notification Laws and Their Effects*, Delft: Delft University of Technology.
9   Bisogni, F. (2020). *Information Availability and Data Breaches. Data Breach Notification Laws and Their Effects*, Delft: Delft University of Technology. (p. 23).

weapons they will sell to which parties. The analogy: a "mandatory reporting on the ultimate beneficiaries of data". Here, the organization that is selling data has to report the identity of the buying party.[10] Again, the rule itself tells us nothing of the content of the data or its use but it does prescribe a procedure. Once more, the assumption is that disclosure obligations provide incentives for organizations to be cautious when passing on data.

Let us now consider a third example of procedural regulation. There are type 3 and type 4 privacy violations; data is being used to manipulate individual users (type 3) or a collective (type 4). Here, bots can play an important role, they can be mistaken for real persons and amplify messages or be used to influence a vote in an election. Substantive regulation of bots is complicated, and procedural regulation is much simpler; California has the 'bot disclosure rule'.[11] The Bot Bill requires bots—or, rather, the parties behind bots—to reveal themselves as a bot in a 'clear, conspicuous, and reasonably designed' manner.

Although the disclosure rule is merely a procedural obligation, it may nevertheless have an impact. When users know they are confronted with a bot, the message loses some of its authenticity. They might understand better if a message was fabricated with the objective of manipulation, or if the bots artificially manufactured the volume of messages.

What is the power of procedural regulation—and what are its limitations?

One. Procedural rules offer both the regulator and the regulatee more decision-making space. When a data breach is reported, clients or the regulator can assess its severity and subsequently

---

10   Howard, P. (2020). *Lie Machines: How to Save Democracy from Troll Armies, Deceitful Robots, Junk News Operations, and Political Operatives*, New Haven: Yale University Press.
11   Noam Cohen (July 2, 2019), *Will California's New Bot Law Strengthen Democracy?*, The New Yorker.

decide how to react to it. As such, procedural rules may contribute to users' empowerment—they are better informed. They may choose to be more critical about the service provider who did not protect their data well.

Two. Although a rule is merely procedural and not substantive, it may be an incentive for data security or privacy. The bot disclosure rule or the mandatory reporting of data breaches may backfire on a company or result in naming and shaming. These perceived risks of procedural regulation can be a strong incentive for companies to do a better job of protecting privacy.

Three. Procedural rules are easier to design than detailed substantive rules. They do not require the differentiation that content-based regulations demand, e.g. taking into account different types of data, types of trade-offs, and types of data breaches. The procedural obligation to perform a privacy review or a Data Protection Impact Assessment is much simpler to design than a more substantive rule. Something similar happens to the enforcement: the mere fact that a bot does not reveal itself or a data breach is not being reported is sufficient grounds for sanctions. The burden of proof will be much simpler than in the case of substantive legislation.

Procedural regulation also has its limitations because it might be based on a number of debatable assumptions.

One. Procedural rules force parties to show their weak sides—and this may be a stimulus for gaming the rules. Companies may downplay the data breach or try to prevent users' attention. Research shows that companies respond to data-breaches with 'no-worries' letters (the letter states that the data-breach poses only a minimal risk), 'junk letters' (letters are crafted in such a way that recipients perceive a letter as being junk mail), or 'routine letters' (the data-breach is presented as inevitable, a more or less customary risk): 'The identified patterns suggest a tendency to trivialize the event (with no worries and junk letter types) when the responsibility of the firm is unquestionable'.[12]

12   Bisogni, F. (2020). *Information Availability and Data Breaches. Data Breach Notification Laws and Their Effects*, Delft: Delft University of Technology. (p. 67).

Two. Not everyone abides by the rules, and this includes procedural rules. In fact, these rules are "merely" procedural, which may even facilitate non-compliance to the rules; a violation of a procedural rule sounds like a procedural mistake and seems less severe than a substantive mistake. Research shows that companies do not report all data leaks.[13] They can frame this as a minor violation, one that can be easily corrected. In reality, refraining from reporting might conceal a data breach, and this can have far-reaching consequences.

Three. Procedural rules can lead to a huge volume of information—about data breaches, bots, selling of data. Sometimes the revealing of this information will already have an impact, for example, when a data breach is being disclosed, the provider's clients may decide against purchasing additional services. But, in many cases, this information will also require follow-up, both from the service providers and from the regulator. When this does not happen (in the case of the regulator this is simply because the regulator lacks the resources to process the notifications), procedural regulation turns into proceduralism—the procedure is followed by companies but is of no further consequence.

4.4   From imposed to negotiated regulation

The ambiguous nature of privacy makes substantive legislation vulnerable ex ante, and there is a subsequent alternative: interaction-based or negotiated regulation. Regulation is not imposed but is the result of a well-designed and structured process of interaction and negotiation.

The basic idea of negotiated rulemaking and negotiated regulation[14] is that involvement of the most important stakeholders in

---

13   Bisogni, F. (2020). *Information Availability and Data Breaches. Data Breach Notification Laws and Their Effects*, Delft: Delft University of Technology. (p. 67).
14   Rulemaking refers to the process of negotiation, and regulation to the outcome of this process.

designing rules is conducive to (1) the quality of and (2) the support for these rules and, as such, beneficial to their executability.[15] Negotiated regulation—Neg Reg—can be found in a variety of fields, from the environment to financial regulation, from healthcare to education. In most cases, the regulation concerns issues that require in-depth and specialized technical or local expertise, which makes the involvement of stakeholders with this expertise necessary. Additionally, regulation may impact the interests of many different actors in a way that is, at times, hard to foresee—and this may also be a reason to negotiate with these parties about the content of the legislation in question.

Negotiated regulation and privacy

Platforms use users' data on a grand scale. This data may be used in an unacceptable manner, and users can be exposed, profiled, or manipulated (type 1–3 violations). It may be unclear what the data is used for, which is also a problem as the data could cause privacy invasions in the future.

There are many parties involved in privacy invasions and possible privacy invasions. For instance, consider type 3 privacy violations. Suppose data is misused to guide users towards increasingly extreme content. Who is responsible for this? The users themselves, of course, but also the producers of the content, the platform leading the user to the content through its algorithms, the co-users who could have warned the user, and, finally, the government, particularly when societal damage may prove considerable whereby type 3 invasions develop into type 4 invasions.

15   C Coglianese, C. (1997). Assessing consensus: The promise and the Performance of Negotiated Rulemaking. *Duke Law Journal, 46,* pp. 1255–1349.; Harter, P. J. (1982). Negotiating regulations: A cure for malaise, *Georgetown Law Journal, 71*(1), pp. 75–91, doi:10.1016/S0195-9255(82)80028-0.; Susskind, L., and McMahon, G. (1985). The Theory and Practice of Negotiated Rulemaking. *Yale Journal on Regulation, 3*(1), pp.133–165.; Ashford, N. A., and Caldart, C. C. (2005). *Negotiated Regulation, Implementation and Compliance in the United States,* New York: Springer.

When such a cooperative responsibility occurs, the consequence may be that representatives of these parties have to collectively determine how serious the problem is and how they should solve it.[16] Cooperative responsibility may entail the development of new buttons in order to cut through bubbles ("You should also read this"), the re-configuration of algorithms, and the possibility of giving users more impact by giving them flagging mechanisms, et cetera. Agreements thereupon can be made in a process of consultation or interaction. If the outcome of this process is codified, we call this result "negotiated regulation".

So, from a government's perspective, negotiated regulation means that a government organizes a process of consultation and negotiation. Key stakeholders are invited to participate in that process. There are other examples of such processes of interaction. Chapter 1 dealt with type 4 privacy violations. An individual is profiled using data (type 2), then manipulated (type 3), and this manipulation can also have consequences for society as a whole (type 4). When it comes to these type 4 privacy violations, the involvement of stakeholders in the development of regulation can be particularly interesting. Let us consider three examples:

First, users with certain profiles are susceptible to fake news (type 3) which can develop into a collective problem (type 4). The question of what is and is not fake is hard to determine by a single party. If information is defined as fake, there is the balancing act between fake and freedom of speech. Not all that is fake is so damaging that its distribution should be prevented. The fake–fact–freedom triangle is unknown and ambiguous territory, and each issue in this triangle can be judged very differently. None of the parties involved in the triangle is capable of solving these issues by themselves, so it makes sense to define the decision making on fake–fact–freedom issues as a cooperative

16   Helberger, N., Pierson, J., and Poell, T. (2018). Governing online platforms: From contested to cooperative responsibility, *The Information Society, 34*(1), pp. 1–14, doi: 10.1080/01972243.2017.1391913.

responsibility.[17] When decision-making concerning the removal of information is left solely to the platforms, it may go wrong, as they may, for example, be too rigorous in monitoring and removing information. Users have a limited influence on these choices—in fact, they can only decide to ignore the fake news. On account of freedom of speech, governments should be inherently hesitant when faced with the tension between fake and freedom. Involving these actors in a process of collective decision making on regulation might be an interesting option.

Second, there are citizen summits on digital surveillance technologies, which have been held in a number of EU member states.[18] First, participants have to be well informed about digital surveillance technologies and become so by studying documents and interacting with experts. Then they debate with one another and with experts, and try to draw conclusions about the use of these technologies. For surveillance technologies, too, there is a wicked triangle consisting of advantages of surveillance (e.g., increased security), the disadvantages (infringement of privacy), and constitutional freedoms (e.g., the freedom of association and assembly). A concrete example here can be seen in tracing apps that are supposed to prevent the spread of Covid-19, but which, of course, also involve significant privacy risks. Public involvement in the use of these apps can play a role in monitoring and limiting these risks.[19]

Third, Apple has developed a software tool for iPhones that can be used to trace images involving the sexual abuse of children.

17   Kaesling, K. (2018). Privatising Law Enforcement in Social Networks: A Comparative Model Analysis. *Erasmus Law Review, 3*, pp. 151–164.

18   Degli Esposti, S., Ball, K., and Dibb, S. (2021). What's In It For Us? *Benevolence, National Security, and Digital Surveillance, Public Administrative Review, 81*(5), pp. 862–873, doi: 10.1111/puar.13362.

19   Alanoca, S., Guetta-Jeanrenaud, N., Ferrari, I., Weinberg, N., Çetin, R. B., and Miailhe, N. (2021). Digital contact tracing against COVID-19: a governance framework to build trust. *International Data Privacy Law, 11*(1), pp. 3–17.; Keller also pleas for more participation-oriented approaches: Keller, P. (2019). The reconstruction of privacy through law: a strategy of diminishing expectations. *International Data Privacy Law, 9*(3), pp. 132–152.

The tool scans codes of images that users upload to ICloudPhotos, before comparing these photos with a database of images from the US National Center for Missing and Exploited Children. If there is a match, an additional check is made and, if the match turns out to be correct, the National Center is informed.

On the one hand, this tool can help fight the evils of child abuse. On the other hand, the technology can also be used (1) to trace other content without the user's consent, which can be undertaken (2) by malicious parties, including malevolent governments.[20] To weigh these two interests, many questions need to be answered:

−   How effective is this tool in recognising images of the sexual abuse of children? Does it only recognize photos that have been modified? Will innocent photos be flagged as child pornography?
−   How effective is the tool in combating child pornography? Will the tool lead to fewer online exchanges of photos and to more accurate detection of offenders? Or will these offenders learn how to bypass the tool?
−   How can this tool be used to discern different content? What are the technical and organizational mechanisms for preventing malicious use of the tool? How reliable are these mechanisms?
−   Can the tool be used by malicious actors for other purposes? How easy is this? Which consequences will this entail?
−   If the tool is used, how can its use and effectiveness be monitored? How transparent is the process of monitoring? What are the possibilities of discontinuing the use of the tool or, alternatively, will discontinuation be very difficult once it has been introduced?

Undoubtedly, there are many more questions that are relevant here. Negotiated rule making can entail organizing a process of interaction, in which the most important stakeholders are

20   Green, M. D., and Stamos, A. (August 11, 2021). *Guest Essay: Apple Wants to Protect Children. But It's Creating Serious Privacy Risks*, New York Times.

involved. This process seeks to answer these and other questions and to reach an agreement on whether and how the tool can be used. Maybe such a process leads to consensus but, even if it does not, it can provide insights that governments (or, in this example, Apple) can use when deciding whether and how to regulate or use the tool. In any case, such a process leads to a broader view of tools like these, than a situation in which parties promptly position themselves as for or against the tool.

Negotiated regulation may require governments' regulation of the process of interaction and negotiation. Such a 'process design' will consist of a set of decision-making rules for the game: Who is invited to deliberate? What is the agenda, how are agreements being created? What is the status of these agreements?[21]

What is the power of negotiated regulation—and what are its limitations?

Privacy protection continuously requires complex trade-offs—between sharing data and services; between fake, fact and freedom; between the quality of current service and the possibility of a privacy violation later on; between individual benefits and collective costs. Some trade-offs can be made upstream, but some can only be made midstream or downstream, when there have been experiences with the different values, the tensions between the values and the possible trade-offs. Negotiated regulation offers room for the parties involved to make these trade-offs when sufficient information is available. The key parties can negotiate a shared trade-off between all the values at stake somewhere during the data-journey. The more these parties are involved, the bigger the chance will be that they will take ownership of the eventual agreements.

What are the limitations of negotiated regulation? First, the assumption of negotiated regulation is that the most important parties are competent and prepared to negotiate with each other

21   de Bruijn, H., ten Heuvelhof, E., and in't Veld, R. (2010). *Process Management*, Berlin: Springer.

in good faith. This assumption is not always correct. Parties may use negotiations to maximize their own interests or frustrate the process because delays are beneficial for them.

Second, the outcome of the negotiation process may reflect the power positions of the parties involved, some parties have more resources (knowledge, money, people) than others and may disproportionately influence the outcome.

Third, this touches on another weakness of negotiated regulation: from the perspective of a government, the outcome of the negotiations may not be good enough, for example, because of such a position of the more powerful parties.

4.5   From direct to indirect regulation

Governments can address regulatees directly, but also indirectly by giving third parties the right or obligation to do so. Governments issue direct regulation against tax evasion: citizens and companies are forbidden to evade taxes and tax evasion results in a financial penalty. Indirect regulation means that government activates a third party to influence the behaviour of these citizens and companies. An example of indirect regulation is the obligation of banks to report cash deposits above a certain amount to the tax authorities, making it more difficult for citizens and companies to conduct large transactions with black money.

Indirect regulation and privacy

There is the example of 'parental deletion rights', which are granted to parents of children under 13 years of age under the US Children's Online Privacy Protection Act. The regulator does not address the regulatee (in this instance, organization in possession of the data) directly but gives third parties (in this case, the parents) the possibility to address them instead.

TikTok—previously known as musical.ly—is a platform where users upload short videos. Every user shares information, including an email address, phone number, full name, username, a profile picture, and a short bio. The videos can be followed and commented upon by others.

Parents in the US may turn to TikTok if they want to exercise their parental deletion rights. A number of parents feel that TikTok is only limitedly responsive when they turn to the company with their complaints. The Federal Trade Commission (FTC), the US privacy watchdog, imposed a heavy sanction on TikTok, following the crucial deliberation that parental consent and deletion rights had been violated: 'The operators of musical.ly—now known as TikTok—knew many children were using the app but they still failed to seek parental consent before collecting names, email addresses, and other personal information from users under the age of 13.'[22] The complaint states that, among other issues, TikTok:

- failed to provide direct notice of its information practices to parents,
- failed to obtain verifiable parental consent prior to collecting, using, and/or disclosing personal information of children, and,
- failed to delete personal information at the request of parents.[23]

The TikTok example shows the effect of indirect regulation: society's eyes and ears are activated through complaining parents, and the mere fact that TikTok violated the parental consent and deletion rights may lead to a conviction.

Both EU and US regulations grant a large number of rights to data subjects. In many cases, these rights can also be interpreted as a form of indirect regulation. The GDPR gives EU citizens the right (1) to be informed about the processing of personal data; (2) access to personal data; (3) to the rectification of incorrect,

22 https://www.ftc.gov/news-events/press-releases/2019/02/video-social-networking-app-musically-agrees-settle-ftc.
23 https://www.ftc.gov/system/files/documents/cases/musical.ly_complaint_ecf_2-27-19.pdf.

inaccurate, or incomplete personal data; (4) to be forgotten; (5) to restrict the processing of data in specific cases; (6) to data portability; (7) to object to the processing of data for marketing purpose; and (8) to demand that high impact decisions based on data are not solely taken by computers, but also by natural persons. The *California Consumer Privacy Act* (CCPA) gives Californians the right (1) to know about the personal information a business collects, uses, and shares; (2) to delete personal information; (3) to opt out of the sale of their personal information; and (4) to non-discrimination for exercising their CCPA rights.[24]

These rights can be activated by citizens and are therefore a form of indirect regulation. In 2020, the Belgian Data Protection Authority sentenced Google to pay a fine due to a violation of the right to be forgotten.[25] The plaintiff (whose name was not disclosed by the Authority) fulfils a public role in Belgium. If you googled the plaintiff's name, you could find a bullying complaint against this person. The complaint had been (1) declared unjustified, was (2) already very old, and (3) may have entailed severe consequences for the plaintiff. Google knew about (1) and (2) and ought to have removed the search results.

The EU regulator does not address Google directly but, through rights within the GDPR, third parties are activated to do so. Again, indirect regulation activates the eyes and ears of society, and implies that companies such as Google do not only face a regulator, but also citizens and companies who have been empowered by legislation.

What is the power of indirect regulation—and what are its limitations?

First and foremost: indirect regulation offers room to weigh privacy and its competing values. In the example above, parents

---

24 *California Consumer Privacy Act* (CCPA).

25 https://www.autoriteprotectiondonnees.be/600.000-euros-damende-lapd-sanctionne-google-belgium-pour-non-respect-du-droit-a-loubli.

are given rights, every parent can make a trade-off between privacy and the importance of TikTok regarding the development of their child. Moreover, today's trade-off between privacy and other values may change tomorrow because parents weigh values differently due to new developments. Indirect regulation can cope with these dynamics. When beliefs about privacy become stricter, rights can be activated. When beliefs become more fluid, parents may waive the activation of their rights.

Second, indirect regulation activates a network of parties who can critically follow a regulatee and, as such, contribute to a system of checks and balances, thereby limiting the power of the regulatee. The stronger these checks and balances are the more responsive a regulatee has to be to the preferences of the individual users. Knowing that these checks and balances might be activated midstream or downstream during the data-journey can motivate the regulatee to think ahead about the trade-off between privacy and other values.

What are the risks of indirect regulation?

The example of TikTok above demonstrates the first risk: the regulatee is sloppy in dealing with third-party requests, in the case of TikTok, the parents' requests. Indirect regulation means that the regulatee is faced with a citizen or a private organization and not with the regulator itself, which might be an incentive for sloppiness. This strategic behaviour is similar to what we saw in the case of the obligation to notify data breaches.

A second risk: indirect regulation presupposes the existence of users who are alert in terms of privacy and its violations, and who possess the competencies to activate their rights. This assumption may turn out to be more accurate in one context than in the other. Many parents of young children will be alert when it comes to their child's privacy. But when, for example, data is being shared and there are split incentives (revenues now, cost in the form of a privacy violation much later, see Chapter 2), there is the risk that indirect regulation will not work.

Closely linked to this is a third risk. Indirect regulation often means that individuals have to take on influential organizations, and this prospect can be a reason for many individuals waiving their rights. Hence, many regulators impose requirements on these organizations, they must establish internal procedures to deal with complaints in a swift manner (see Section 8 below).

4.6   From instrumental to institutional regulation

A football association has an interest in football being an attractive and exciting sport. When footballers pass the ball to their goalkeeper too often, and thereby make football less attractive, football associations can intervene by changing the rules of the game. They can, for example, introduce a back-pass rule whereby goalkeepers are forbidden to handle the ball when passed to them by a team-mate. The idea is that new rules will lead to new interactions between actors (in this case, the football players). A change in the rules of the game can have a major impact, but obviously cannot be undertaken too often.

Institutions are 'rules that structure social interactions'.[26] In more everyday language, institutions are also referred to as the "rules of the game"[27]—rules that are fixed for a long time, and which regulate behaviour between social actors, just like the rules of a sport. There are informal and formal institutions, and the latter include all those institutions that are laid down in legislation.

The regulation discussed so far is aimed at privacy protection. This is why we speak of instrumental regulation, because the rule is an instrument used to promote privacy protection.

---

26   Hodgson, G. M. (2006). What are Institutions? *Journal of Economic Issues*, 40(1), pp. 1–25.
27   North, D. C. (1990). *Institutions, Institutional Change and Economic Performance*. Cambridge. Cambridge University Press.

Privacy can also be protected by changing the underlying rules of the game in a society, which is referred to as institutional regulation.

Institutional regulation and privacy

In Australia, a teenage prisoner was treated in a degrading way and a picture of this treatment was posted on the Internet by various media companies. These companies offered readers the opportunity to comment on the photo, which lead to many defamatory comments. It is an example of a type 1 privacy invasion: a personal photo is made public, and the teenager is then the victim of further public humiliation due to the ubiquity of the Internet. The question then arose as to which individual is legally responsible for this, to which the answer could be given that is the people who posted the defamatory comments.

The High Court of Australia decided that the media companies can also be held liable for the comments that their readers post: 'By the creation of a public Facebook page and the posting of content on that page', the media companies 'facilitated, encouraged and thereby assisted the publication of comments from third-party Facebook users. The [media companies] were therefore publishers of the third-party comments.'[28]

This is an example of institutional regulation. The rules of the game are changed: media companies are made liable for hateful and offensive comments posted by others under their coverage. They have a "publisher liability".

This decision has a potentially far-reaching impact. Because media companies are liable, they will make an effort to prevent hateful and offensive comments, for example by moderating more actively or by turning off the "comments" function. This means that the privacy violation journey will be halted or at the very made more difficult.

28   https://cdn.hcourt.gov.au/assets/publications/judgment-summaries/2021/hca-27-2021-09-08.pdf

Section 230 of the *United States Communications Decency Act* reads as follows:

> No provider or user of an interactive computer service shall be treated as the publisher or speaker of any information provided by another information content provider.

Section 230 protects platforms, which are not legally responsible for the content that others post on the platform. As such, they differ from publishers and have no "publisher liability"; if they did, they probably could hardly exist or, if they did exist, would be less innovative. Because of this protection, platforms can be a haven for hate speech, fake news, or conspiracy theories, and they can facilitate privacy violations. Think here of type 1 violations (sensitive private information is posted on a platform and gets a huge reach), but also of type 2, 3, and 4 violations (platforms can be a hotbed of fake news, and platforms' algorithms can connect this fake news to users with a certain profile).

Section 230 could be changed. One option, for instance, would be to maintain the protection for "publisher liability", but to introduce a "distributor liability". This would mean that a platform would have no legal responsibility for the content of posts, but it would have legal responsibility for their distribution. This could offer the possibility to forbid "algorithmic amplification": using algorithms to spread a message on a large scale.[29] This too would be a form of institutional regulation and, like the Australian High Court ruling, it too could have far-reaching consequences.

What is the difference between, say, procedural regulation and indirect regulation on the one hand and institutional regulation on the other? Take the obligation to notify data breaches (procedural regulation) and parental deletion rights (indirect regulation).

29 Lindsay, R. (October 27, 2020). To Fix Section 230, Target Algorithmic Amplification, The Information.

Both forms of regulation are aimed at protecting privacy. Institutional regulation is about the underlying rules of the game. For both data breach notifications and parental deletion rights, it makes quite a difference whether a platform has publisher liability or not. Suppose that confidential information has been obtained from a data breach and that this information is posted on a platform. If that platform has a publisher liability (institutional regulation), the position of the victim of the breach is stronger than it would be without this liability. Something similar applies to parental deletion rights: the position of parents becomes stronger if platforms are not allowed to post incorrect content.

What is the strength of institutional regulation—and what are the risks?

The strength is that a structural change takes place: the rules of the game are changed, something that can have far-reaching consequences for privacy protection. When media companies become legally responsible for third-party comments they must make structural decisions to prevent themselves from being held liable for hateful content.

Moreover, as mentioned above, when the rules of the game change, the other forms of regulation may be more effective.

The power of institutional regulation is also its risk. Privacy always stands in relation to another value; in the example of Section 230 this is, at the very least, innovation and freedom of speech. The structural nature of institutional interventions can also mean that these values are severely eroded. Moreover, the impact of institutional regulation is not always predictable. The best case would be that it leads to more protection of privacy, while the worst case would be that it has to great an effect on the competing values (innovation, freedom of speech) too much. Institutional change is not always easy to reverse and that is a problem if the intended change has many negative and unforeseen effects.

4.7 The essence of resilience-based regulation

To sum up, privacy is a process (Chapter 1), and privacy protection is a wicked issue—one that is characterized by ambiguity, emergence, variety, and dynamics (see Chapter 2). These characteristics require resilient governance, in two different senses: (1) governance is a process, one that covers the entire data-journey, from upstream to downstream; and (2) governance requires redundancy—a variety of incentives for privacy protection.

Resilience and the power of the state

This chapter addresses the power of the state. Goal-based regulation, procedural regulation, negotiated regulation, and indirect regulation offer space for regulators and regulatees to make midstream or downstream trade-offs and to cope with the following:
- Ambiguity: the need for trade-offs between privacy and other values.
- Uncertainty: dealing with privacy issues that emerge during the data-journey.
- Variety: dealing with the variety of different situations.
- Dynamics: changes during the data-journey.

Institutional regulation changes the underlying rules of the game, and this can be conducive to the effective application of the other forms of regulation (see the example of data breaches and parental deletion rights).

Using the whole set of legal instruments also creates a certain redundancy: there is a large number of incentives to protect privacy. Moreover, the room these tools offer can activate and empower users and service providers, thereby contributing to redundancy because more actors are more alert regarding the value of privacy. Subsequently a network of checks and balances may emerge.

In this Chapter, I have paid much attention to the family of legal instruments. Hopefully, it will have become clear from the examples that financial and communicative instruments are also important. Take the example of TikTok and parental deletion rights mentioned above. Not respecting those rights can lead to high fines (financial instruments) and, of course, the FTC provides a lot of information on parental deletion rights (communication instruments).

The role of upstream interventions

The focus in this chapter lay heavily on resilience as midstream and downstream interventions. By not intervening too early in data-journeys, space is created to make trade-offs during these journeys. Each type of of regulation offers that space. However, the importance of midstream and downstream interventions does not mean that upstream regulation is unimportant. In fact, the effectiveness of midstream and downstream interventions is strongly dependent on upstream regulation.

Take, for example, Article 5.1 of the GDPR[30] that codifies the well-known principles for data protection (see Chapter 1). Without these principles, there is no legal ground and no framework for interventions either midstream or downstream. The principles regarding data protection are a *sine qua non* for effective interventions midstream or downstream.

Ex ante regulation may also function as the "shadow of the law" and, as such, create disincentives for opportunistic behaviour of the regulatee. The use of the shadow of the law can be found in several other domains, including environmental regulation. Governmental and industrial actors may negotiate the required environmental demands on businesses in order to come to "negotiated regulation". Governments may bolster their position in these negotiations through the use of unilateral regulation as a fall-back scenario. In the event that negotiations fall through, this fall-back scenario can be activated, and

---

30 'Personal data shall be processed in a manner that ensures appropriate security of the personal data'.

the desired environmental performance can be unilaterally imposed. The shadow of the law hangs over the negotiation table; if no agreement is made today, unilateral regulation may be deployed tomorrow. When this is applied to the world of data and privacy, (1) there are regulatory tools in place, (2) which a government does not use if resilience-based regulation leads to desired results, and, furthermore, (3) does use when this is not the case.

The threat of new regulation can also cast a shadow over regulatees. In 2020, the European Parliament supported a proposition that forbids personalized advertising. The main arguments are that business models, based on personalized advertising, are a strong stimulus for gathering data, which spoils the advert market for other parties and generates too much market power for tech giants. A ban on personalized advertising could potentially impact the essence of the tech giants' business model. The proposed ban can be interpreted as a shadow of the law—when companies no longer exert themselves to prevent privacy violations, the ultimate consequence may be a complete prohibition of personal advertisements in Europe.

Thus, downstream regulation can only be effective when there is also upstream, ex ante regulation. Resilience-based regulation without ex ante regulation leads to too much space and incentives for opportunism.

4.8 Conditions for regulation based on resilience— capacity and infrastructure building

The space offered by resilience-based regulations also places demands on the organizations involved. Firstly, there is the need for capacity building, and organizations must acquire the skills and expertise to handle this decision-making space properly. Secondly, there is the need for infrastructure building and the designing of structures conducive to the proper use of regulation that protects privacy.

Capacity building

Organizations and individuals need to be sufficiently competent in order to use the space that resilience offers. For example, goal-based regulation in healthcare assumes that involved healthcare professionals can make a trade-off between care, privacy, and other values, even when this may imply that a physician's work becomes less efficient. Moreover, the parties involved must have a sufficient sense of urgency where the value of privacy is concerned; when the importance of this value is not acknowledged it will be subject to being perpetually overpowered.

Infrastructure building

Regulation as resilience entails a series of infrastructural consequences. First, resilience makes significant demands on the structure of the organizations involved. The *Children's Online Privacy Protection Act* determines that a service provider 'must make reasonable efforts to obtain verifiable parental consent, taking into consideration available technology'[31]—for instance, a consent form to be signed by the parent or a toll-free telephone number and video conference facility for parents, one that is staffed by trained personnel.[32] Without any such provisions, parents have a more challenging time exercising their deletion rights.

The GDPR obliges certain organizations to appoint data protection officers (DPOs). A DPO monitors whether privacy is properly secured, gives advice, and is a point of contact for employees. The DPO should have access to the highest level of management. In response to the Cambridge Analytica scandal, the FTC has commanded Facebook appoints compliance

---

31   Children's Online Privacy Protection Rule, Section 321.5
32   Federal Trade Commission (2020), *Complying with COPPA: FAQs*, https://www.ftc.gov/tips-advice/business-center/guidance/complying-coppa-frequently-asked-questions-0, July

officers responsible for implementing Facebook's privacy program.[33]

An entirely different example: negotiated knowledge means that negotiations are being undertaken by an individual for an organization with other organizations. This may imply that the organization designs mandate schemes, negotiators should have the right mandate and information, to negotiate effectively.

Second, the decision-making space, inherent to resilience-based regulation, requires a regular reflection on the part of involved actors. How is this space used? Are there any patterns in the way these actors deal with this space? What are the main issues, the main disputes, and the main uncertainties? It is essential that this process of evaluation and reflection is well organized to identify and codify the main lessons learned. When organizations execute these processes regularly, the space resilience offers can be used to a greater degree.

Third, almost all tech giants have given external advisors a role in decision-making processes; Google has an Advanced Technology External Advisory Council, Facebook a Safety Advisory Board, and Twitter a Trust and Safety Council. External advisors are supposed to be a countervailing power within the organization, and the rules of play regarding their advice are essential here. There are several important questions to consider: Is advice is only solicited or is it also unsolicited? Is the advice confidential or public? Does the board of a company have an obligation to respond to the advice or not?

Fourth, the space that goal-based regulation offers also requires accountability in terms of how this space is used. How has the room been used? Does resilience result in too much room and too many incentives for opportunism, or does it contribute to better privacy protection? Accordingly, processes of accountability have to be put in place.

---

33   Murphy, L. W., and Cacace, M. (2020). *Facebook's civil rights audit – Final report*. https://about.fb.com/wp-content/uploads/2020/07/Civil-Rights-Audit-Final-Report.pdf

Governments can use the power of the state to protect privacy, but the power of the market is also important. The free market of data-based services is a problem for many when it comes to privacy. However, governments can also use the power of the market to protect privacy. This is the subject of Chapter 5

5   The Power of the Market

5.1   Introduction

How can the market contribute to more privacy protection?

Here, the first observation has to be that the market is part of the problem. For decades, free, under-regulated markets have been an ideal breeding ground for the massive and continuous harvesting of data—the Cambridge Analytica scandal is an iconic example of the consequences of this phenomenon. However, the market may also be part of the solution. In this chapter, I will discuss a number of these market-based solutions:

- Competing on privacy: privacy protection may be part of companies' propositions, with which they differentiate themselves from other service providers. When privacy is being competed on, incentives may arise for companies to increasingly invest into privacy protection simply to keep up with their competitors (Section 2).
- Pricing and taxing data: through pricing or taxing data, financial incentives may occur that result in there being reduced demand for data. Less demand for data may reduce the risk of privacy violations (Section 3).
- Opening the black box of the business propositions of companies, thereby enabling more transparency of the use of data and, in particular, the effectiveness of the data use. Is data-driven service always as vital and effective as is suggested (Section 4)?
- Cutting up the data-journey, or even breaking up companies. This will create a series of barriers, so, during its journey, data will be faced with these barriers; the more barriers, the more opportunities for privacy protection (Section 5).

Using the power of the market still requires a role from governments. Some of the solutions presented in this chapter, presuppose government intervention. Others will emerge on the market but can be facilitated or fuelled through government interventions. Section 6 connects the four market-based solutions to the concept of resilient governance.

5.2 Competing on privacy

In a market, companies compete on pricing or quality, but they can also compete on privacy. Then, in that company's business proposition, privacy has an important place. This may result in more demand for their services. Incidentally, the economic value of their data may also increase—the less traceable the data is to persons, the easier it is to sell this to third parties.

Competition and privacy

Competition on privacy can arise in many markets—here are some important examples.

Competition between search engines. People who use a search engine share data, data that can easily be linked to an IP address and then used for profiling. When, subsequently, someone ends up on a company's website via such a search engine, a data transaction may take place between the search engine and the company. For instance, the search engine could communicate to the company which search queries have been used by what IP address.

A search engine may also choose not to do this and present itself as more privacy friendly. DuckDuckGo does not store IP addresses and does not build up any user profiles (type 2 privacy invasion) and, therefore, DuckDuckGo's recommendations are less biased (type 3 and type 4 privacy invasions). Information that the search engine does not have can simply not be passed on to third parties. There is, of course, a downside: whoever uses a search engine "pays" with data and gets high-quality search results in return. More privacy can result in lower-quality search results.

Competition between web-browsers.[1] Companies offering browsers have entirely different interests. For Google (Google Chrome), the interest lies in the use of user data for the advertising engine. For Apple (Safari), the interest lies in consumer loyalty to the iPhone, preventing users from moving to Android. Mozilla is a not-for-profit organization that developed the Firefox browser and, as such, has no interest in the harvesting of data. This means that Firefox is much more privacy-friendly and has a number of important features that are directed towards privacy protection. Additionally, the web-browser is fully open source —everyone can check the source code, which is also interesting from a privacy perspective.

There are other examples of competition on privacy:
–   between ISPs (the ISP "Freedom Internet" has a strong focus on privacy and is a non-profit ISP, competing with commercial enterprises);
–   between operating systems (Apple iOS versus Google Android);
–   between apps that provide similar services, or between all kinds of online services (e.g., video-calling systems);
–   between system layers, for example, between exchange platforms and maker platforms (Facebook is an "exchange platform" that runs on "maker platforms", for instance, on Apple, therefore, when Facebook handles apps that conflict with Apple's privacy rules, Apple can block them or disable certain technical features.[2]

The impact of competition on privacy

Market competition is currently often limited because there are dominant players in the market. The search engine market, for example, is dominated by Google (which has a market share of

1   Hern, A. (November 17, 2019). *Firefox's fight for the future of the web*, The Guardian.
2   Isaac, M. (January 13, 2019). *Apple Shows Facebook Who Has the Power in an App Dispute*, The New York Times.

approx. 90%), and the browser market by Google Chrome and Safari (market shares of approx. 65% and 20%, respectively).

Competitors such as DuckDuckGo (search engine) and Firefox (browser) have a more privacy-friendly proposition, but their market-share is small (DuckDuckGo at 0.5%, Firefox at 5%). Competition can still can have an effect, not just when the competitors are big players but also when they are small, niche players. I identify the following functions.

Voicing privacy-invasions. Even niche players such as Duck-DuckGo may play an important role because they articulate the worries that customers have about big players, for instance, when a search engine games its search results for marketing reasons, bombards users with ads, or follows them. Niche players can be the thorn in the flesh of the key players.

Creating technological countervailing powers. Privacy-friendly competitors continuously explore technological options to better protect privacy and show that there are alternatives to the propositions of less privacy-friendly companies. Firefox is proof that you can build browsers that do not aggregate data. DuckDuckGo shows that search engines can be privacy-proof. Often, small players are more open-source oriented than the big players. Furthermore, when the innovations of these small parties work, big companies may be more or less forced to adopt them.

Creating transparency. The first two functions automatically lead to more transparency. Privacy violations occur within an arcane web of technology and economic interests, which is also extremely dynamic. When companies compete for privacy, this also leads to greater insight into what the possibilities for privacy protection are and, therefore, to greater insight regarding where other companies cross the line.

Challenging big tech's business models. Service providers that showcase themselves with privacy often have a completely different business model than their competitors. DuckDuckGo and Firefox may forego the massive harvesting of data because their business model does not require them to do so. This means that they challenge their competitors' business model and, as such, are even a potentially bigger threat because the core values of the data giants are at stake. When service provision is possible with a different business model, these incumbents may become more vulnerable—for example, because governments have less difficulty intervening, to the detriment of an incumbent.

Attracting attention and support from third parties. In sectors in which quality is a concept that is both complex and difficult to understand, we often see the emergence of benchmarks and rankings that can help consumers in their choice of provider. In the world of digital services, quality is also difficult to grasp and understand. The more competition, the more mature a market becomes, the greater the chance that benchmarks and rankings will emerge here too. For instance, Germany's cyber-security agency, the Bundesamt für Sicherheit in der Informationstechnik (BSI), carried out an audit of browsers and rated Firefox as the most secure browser.[3] The goal of these investigations is to advise government agencies and companies about the use of browsers. When a third party, such as a cybersecurity agency, makes these recommendations, this can obviously strengthen the position of a browser.

In conclusion, therefore, it can be said that although small competitors have important disadvantages when compared with the big players, they may nevertheless play an interesting role. A metaphor that comes to mind here is the that of "hibernator". One competitor in sleep mode is not much of a threat, but when there are "hibernators" everywhere, one of them might wake up

3   Cimpanu, C. (October 17, 2019). *Germany's cyber-security agency recommends Firefox as most secure browser,* ZDNet. (Not all existing browsers were included in the audit).

and become a serious competitor for the big players. Another metaphor that can be used here is that of the 16th century Spanish Armada: a fleet of big ships that are vulnerable to small, agile boats when surrounded by them.

What role can government play?

Companies compete on privacy and thus the role of governments is limited, however, governments can indeed be a catalyst for competing on privacy. How?

First, attention to privacy can be a breeding ground for privacy-based competition. The mere fact that governments promote the value of privacy, protect privacy by law, and warn citizens about the impact of privacy-violations creates a breeding ground for competing on privacy. The more societal attention to and concerns about privacy, the more appealing it is for companies to differentiate from others with the value of privacy.

Second, governments can facilitate competition on privacy. An example was mentioned earlier, specifically, browser ranking by the German cybersecurity agency. In environmental policies, certification is a well-known tool. Companies that meet certain environmental demands can obtain certification, providing consumers certainty about the level of environmental performance of a product, service, or company. Something similar is possible in the world of data and privacy. The EU–US Privacy Shield, an agreement between the EU and the US, comprises rules for US companies that process European personal data. Companies that meet the requirements of the Privacy Shield receive a certificate.[4] A company that is in possession of a certificate has committed to very strict conditions for sharing data to third parties, is regularly checked by the regulator regarding this commitment, and may, if they violate the commitment conditions, also lose their certificate. Although the Court of Justice of the EU declared

4   For the list of Privacy Shield participants, see: https://www.privacyshield.gov/list.

the Privacy Shield invalid in 2020[5] because it is not sufficiently in line with the GDPR, the idea of such an instrument or quality mark is of course still valuable.

Third, governments can be launching customers. Governmental agencies may opt for a video-calling system that offers the most privacy and solely communicate via this system.

Finally, governments can protect the level of competition and prevent markets from developing into oligopolies with a limited number of dominant players (see Section 5).

5.3 The pricing and taxing of data

In the world of data, there exists the business model according to which customers get a free service and pay with their data and attention in return. This business model has an important implication: it has no financial incentives to limit the harvesting of data. Companies can obtain data for free and clients are given better service in return—assuming they provide the data for free. This simple observation leads to an interesting question: When a company is charged for data, is this a disincentive for the gathering of data? There are two options here:

– taxing, whereby governments can introduce a data tax, or
– pricing, whereby service providers, individual users, or a collective of users can agree about a compensation for the collection or use of data.

The arguments for and against pricing and taxing

There are a number of arguments in favour of a data tax that have little to do with privacy deliberations. The most important being that data giants have a strong impetus to establish head offices in

---

5   Court of Justice of the European Union (16 July 2020), Judgment of the Court, Case C-311/18. https://curia.europa.eu/juris/document/document.jsf?text=&docid=2286 77&pageIndex=0&doclang=en&mode=lst&dir=&occ=first&part=1&cid=10784871

low-tax countries (in, for instance, Ireland), while value is being created in others. This disconnect between physical location and value creation means that value creation takes place with the data of citizens outside of the low-tax country. This is unfair and may legitimize a data tax: the country in which the value is created, imposes a tax on data-harvesting companies.[6] However, in this book, I focus on data tax as an instrument to strengthen privacy-protection.

What are the arguments in favour of pricing or taxing data?
– When data is to be paid for, this may provide a financial incentive to gather less data since data will become an expense and will have to have value before a company pays for it. These payments will often only be small amounts, but for companies that harvest data on a large scale, there still may be a financial incentive for less data gathering.[7]
– Pricing and taxing can contribute to user awareness and empowerment. Users of services will perhaps be more alert and will better inform themselves about data collection and release.[8]
– Pricing and taxing imply that new legal relations occur between government and companies that collect data (taxing) or between users and the data-collectors (pricing). These relations come with an important by-catch—there will be more ties between these parties and these ties can be used as communication channels for other issues.[9]

6   European Commission (2018). *Proposal for a Council Directive laying down rules relating to the corporate taxation*, Brussels.
7   Rubinstein, Z. (2021). Taxing Big Data: A Proposal to Benefit Society for the Use of Private Information. *Fordham Intellectual Property, Media and Entertainment Law Journal, 31*(4), pp. 1241–1244.
8   Gianclaudio, M., and Custers, B. (2018). Pricing privacy – the right to know the value of your personal data, Computer law and Security Review, *34*(2), pp. 289–303.
9   Rubinstein, Z. (2021). Taxing Big Data: A Proposal to Benefit Society for the Use of Private Information. *Fordham Intellectual Property, Media and Entertainment Law Journal, 31*(4), pp. 1241–1244.

- When this idea is introduced on a massive scale, a new service-providing industry may emerge, which takes care of financial transactions on behalf of users, and which also represents users' interests. This too is a form of user empowerment.
- From a normative perspective, pricing and taxing might also be desirable. Companies make a lot of money with data, so it is only reasonable that they pay for it through taxing or a compensation to the user.

And then there are the arguments against pricing or taxing data.
- Data only has value when it is combined with other data, so the value of an individual data-dot is quite difficult to determine, which makes both the level of taxation and the price fairly arbitrary.[10]
- This is particularly true when data is widely available. The higher the supply, the lower the price, so it is very likely that the value of a data-dot will be negligible.[11]
- People have data about other people. Think of data about a person's network or a person's whereabouts, which may also point to the whereabouts of others. This raises the question as to who should receive the compensation?[12]
- Then there is the question as to what happens with data when payment is being made through taxing or compensation. Does that mean that users lose their claim on the data? Even when, later on, this becomes much more valuable, through unanticipated use? Even when it is used for privacy invasions?

---

10   Wadhwa, T. (2020). *Economic Impact and Feasibility of Data Dividends*, Washington DC: Data Catalyst. (p. 5).

11   Oremus, W. (2019). *How Much Is Your Privacy Really Worth?* OneZero. https://onezero.medium.com/how-much-is-your-privacy-really-worth-421796dd9220.

12   Priest, D. (n. d.). *Google and Facebook treating your data like property would be terrible – CNET.* https://www.cnet.com/news/google-and-facebook-treating-your-data-like-property-would-be-terrible/.

- The transaction costs for compensating data may outweigh the benefits. The price and volume of data are so low that the money transfer is more expensive.
- Then finally, there is the normative objection that privacy is a right and that, by paying for data, it seems that this right is tradeable. The ultimate consequence might be that whoever needs money has to sell data, and thus relinquishes a right, and, comparatively, whoever has deep pockets, does not have to do so.[13]

Of course, these objections are partly rebuttable. The technology exists to minimize transaction costs, and selling data can be subject to limitation so as not to infringe upon the right to privacy. Not all data is suitable for compensation, but this does not mean that this mode of thinking is a dead end. Moreover, these objections apply in cases of private compensation, rather than public taxing, so letting companies pay for data does not need to be categorically rejected. I will further explore both directions: pricing and taxing.

Homogeneous and heterogeneous datasets

The price of a single data point is difficult to determine, but the pricing of datasets might be easier. Here, we can distinguish between homogeneous and heterogeneous datasets.

A homogeneous dataset is a set of similar data, so the user knows which data is being shared and, often, what the data is used for. Examples are the data on purchasing behaviour or travel behaviour via loyalty programmes, or data collected by a device that is connected to the Internet (driving behaviour, sports activities, patterns in the use of certain devices). In a heterogeneous dataset, the variety of types of data is greater and it is inherently less clear what the data is being used for. The example here is, of course, the variety of data that Facebook collects.

13   Wadhwa, T. (2020). *Economic Impact and Feasibility of Data Dividends*, Washington DC: Data Catalyst. (pp. 6–7).

Pricing and homogenous datasets

The more homogeneous a dataset is, the more it can be seen as a commodity, one that can be traded and priced. In fact, companies are already paying for this kind of data. Let us consider three examples:

- Membership cards. Through membership-cards, users hand over data about the products and services they buy from a particular supplier, plus a number of personal details. Thanks to the data, the service provider can develop a better marketing-, sales-, or distribution-strategy. Companies can easily stipulate a price for the handing over of this particular data—those individuals who relinquish data through their membership-card are often given discounts in return.
- Navigation services. Car owners may gather data about road conditions, such as data concerning traffic jams and potholes. When this data is being handed over, it may be used to improve the quality of navigation services. This service can be regarded as a compensation for relinquishing data but, nevertheless, there may still be room for a remuneration to the data provider. Jaguar Land Rover has a project, whereby car owners are paid for their sharing of data about congestion, accidents, or the quality of the road surface—in the form of crypto-currency and a smart wallet.
- Lifestyle insurances. These are insurances that use lifestyle data, which is gathered by users through apps. For example, step counters or apps that record sports activities. Insurance companies are interested in this data and may offer users discounts on their insurance premium provided they (1) relinquish this data and (2) the data shows that they reach a certain level of physical activity.

Suppose that this kind of development continues and that homogeneous datasets will be paid for—can this be an incentive for less data-sharing and, therefore, for more privacy-protection? The assumption here is that a higher price for data will lead to less demand for data. However, this assumption is, of course, disputable.

Firstly, the impact of the financial incentive on data collection will depend on a series of additional variables. Let us consider three examples:

- Substitutes? Does the data-harvesting company have a substitute; i.e., can it switch to other data or information that fulfils a similar or equivalent function, and which has no price? If so, pricing will increase the odds that the company switches to the substitute and, subsequently, two situations may occur:
  - The substitute-data that replace the priced data may be used to invade privacy—pricing aimed at privacy protection creates substitution effects, resulting in a privacy invasion elsewhere.
  - The substitute-data that replace the priced data has less impact on privacy. Pricing could result in less data collection and use. Although pricing results in substitution, not in less data use, it still is conducive to privacy protection.
- Innovation? Are there opportunities for innovation? If service providers must pay for data, are there technical and economic opportunities by which they can innovate and make their services less data-dependent? If so, data pricing may lead to more privacy protection. If not, data pricing may lead to revenues for the user, but not to incentives for more privacy protection.
- Core? There is also the simple question as to what the role of data is. Is it crucial to the services companies provide? Is it at the core of their business models? In the latter case, of course, the incentive for less data collection is weaker than it is when data is not crucial.

Secondly, due to pricing, data may become a business model for users. Put simply, they can earn money by making their data available to others, which makes pricing an incentive for sharing data and compromising privacy rather than a disincentive. In addition to this, the literature on performance management teaches us that financial incentives almost always come with perverse effects, including 'gaming the numbers'.[14] Data pricing can also be an incentive for users to manipulate data and thus make money.[15]

Still, this reasoning should come with an important annotation. Again, privacy is an ambiguous concept, and opposite sharing data there is a "competing value" in the form of better service. This has a consequence regarding the judgement of privacy. Take the lifestyle insurance again, a first assessment may be as follows: a lifestyle insurance is a strong impetus to hand over data, and as such, it is not beneficial for the protection of privacy.

The second assessment is different. Suppose that the remuneration for data (for example, a lower premium) is not solely an incentive to hand over data but also incentivizes a healthy lifestyle, and that, furthermore, healthy lifestyles are highly prioritized in society. This may lead to a wholly different assessment. The first judgment is based on two considerations: there is a financial compensation and there is the handing over of data. The second judgment is based on three considerations: compensation, handing over data, and a healthier lifestyle. The conclusion may be that pricing leads to new services (healthier lifestyle), that these services are highly valued, and that this justifies the handing over of data.

This second assessment is rather paradoxical. Privacy is an ambiguous concept and always exists opposite other values, in this case, health. Data pricing may come hand in hand with new types of service provision and will, therefore, require requires a new weighing. The paradox is as follows: pricing leads to increased data-sharing, but not to a more negative assessment in terms of privacy-protection due to this new, valuable service.

14   de Bruijn, H. (2006). *Managing Performance in the Public Sector*, London: Routledge. (pp. 19–24).
15   Bax, E. (2019). *Computing A Data Dividend*. ACM Economics & Computation 2019, https://arxiv.org/pdf/1905.01805.pdf

I recall an important observation about resilience mentioned in Chapter 3. When privacy is violated, resilience may entail restoring the old situation, but resilience may also point to a new balance between privacy and other values. Here, we see this rebalancing: data pricing leads to new incentives, both for data-sharing and for new services and, therefore, leads to a new equilibrium.

Taxing and heterogeneous datasets

A heterogeneous dataset will be similar to the data collected by Facebook. It encompasses all aspects of life and is being gathered in many different ways. This data is subsequently being processed and used for certain services, and it is not always clear upfront for which services the data will be used or who the services will benefit. This means that commoditization of data is much harder and, additionally, that pricing is more difficult. This can be quite unsatisfactory, given the enormous financial value of aggregated data.

What is the way out? When the value of individual data is hard to assess, but there is huge financial gain at an aggregated level, the remuneration for this data could happen happen at a collective level, not at an individual level. There are several analogies supporting this idea.

Levies and externalities. In environmental economics we find the concept of "externalities"—the damaging impact an economic activity has on the environment. Such environmental damage is not part of the economic cost–benefit analysis of a company; the benefits of an economic activity concern the company, the costs of the environmental damage concern society as a whole. Environmental taxes, such as eco-levies, are important instruments for dealing with these externalities. Sometimes, these taxes work as a financial incentive to decrease externalities, sometimes they work as remuneration used by governments to invest in the environment, and sometimes the tax has both functions.

Gathering data is also subject to externalities, including loss of privacy, the spread of fake news, the corrosion of the democratic processes. When the gathering of data entails externalities as a consequence, a data tax may be considered.

Funds with income from natural resources. Resource-rich countries have sovereign wealth funds. Revenues from these resources are deposited in a fund and are subsequently used to make investments in society and the economy. For example, Norway has high revenues from oil, and deposits these revenues in the Government Pension Fund Global. The Fund does not invest in ecologically irresponsible projects. There is an interesting paradox here: the revenues stem from oil, but the investments are green. The comparison with taxing data is obvious: data tax income can be used to create a fund, and investments by this fund can, for example, be focused on the development of privacy enhancing technologies. A variant of this can be seen in the following example: Facebook's co-founder Chris Hughes also advocates a data tax and uses the Permanent Fund of the State of Alaska as an analogy—oil companies deposit part of their revenue in the fund, which subsequently passes part of the income on to Alaskans.[16] In recent years payment was approximately $1600 per inhabitant.[17] This can be more than a money cheque for citizens—if the tax is linked to the volume of data collected, it can also be an incentive to collect less data.

Users' self-organization. In these two analogies, governments are the active party. But it is also possible that users organize themselves into a collective. There are three interesting analogies here:
- Unions. In many sectors, individual employees do not have a strong position to negotiate with employers, unions do, and

---

16   Marian, O. Y. (2021). Taxing Data. *UC Irvine School of Law Research Paper Series*, *17*, pp. 53–54.
17   Hughes, C. (April 27, 2018). *The wealth of our collective data should belong to all of us*, The Guardian.

therefore negotiate the working conditions with employers. In some cases, "data agents" may negotiate the price for the availability and use of data on behalf of the data providers.

– Patients' associations. Patients' associations represent people afflicted by a particular illness. They could also negotiate the price of data, albeit for their highly specific target group. The price is the result of negotiation, rather than regulation. Accordingly, an agent can vary the price and demand a higher price from pharma companies than from non-commercial medical researchers.

– Purchasing associations. Within a purchasing organization, buyers collaborate, for example, when stipulating collective discounts with suppliers. A company can offer a data-intensive service, and buyers can unite in order to bargain for discounts on this particular service since they are the data-suppliers who determine the quality of this service. Again, it is a somewhat ambiguous situation and setting the "right" price is not easy. If there is no right price, a negotiated price might be an interesting alternative, something that requires buyers working together in an association.

Do these forms of tax lead to less demand for data and less privacy invasions? The effect of taxing will primarily depend on the criteria for taxation.

As already discussed above, if there is a direct relation between the volume of the harvested data and the tax, the tax might be an incentive to gather less data, although the considerations mentioned in the previous paragraphs also play a role here (substitutes or not, innovation potential or not, data are at the core or periphery of the business model).

When there is no direct relation with data harvesting, for example, the tax is a percentage of companies' turnover or profit, the incentive for less harvesting of data will be much weaker. Rather, the tax functions as compensation for sharing data, or can be used to invest in privacy enhancing technologies.

What roles can government play?

Of course, government can introduce taxes or facilitate pricing, but there is more.

First, there is the legal–normative issue of privacy being a right. Through pricing, this right is turned into a commodity. This may, in a normative sense, be undesirable, because the importance of supplementary income may vary according to someone's financial situation and, as such, one person can afford the right to privacy, while another cannot.

In addition, financial incentives such as pricing can even suppress moral considerations. When someone does something on moral grounds, and subsequently receives a reward for this action, a reward that might expire over time, there is the risk that moral considerations do not reappear.[18] The rationality of the financial transaction therefore becomes more important than the rationality of the moral consideration.

Applied to privacy and data, this could mean that data pricing may outrank the moral considerations that privacy is a fundamental right. This presents an important role for government, it makes sure that data pricing does not compromise the right to privacy. Getting paid for data concerning, for example, travel behaviour, should only be possible within a regulatory framework that protects car drivers' privacy. Legal principles such as data minimization and purpose limitation still apply, and data may only be paid for if it has been collected in accordance with these principles. There is another paradox here: the market mechanism of pricing can only work properly when there is government regulation that sufficiently protects privacy.

Second, pricing may have a positive impact on privacy, yet it may also come with a perverse effect, namely, incentives for users to relinquish more data. This may also require government interventions—certain forms of pricing are permitted, others are

18   de Bruijn, H. (2006). *Managing Performance in the Public Sector*, London: Routledge. (pp. 19–24).

not. The distinction between homogeneous datasets (individual pricing possible) and heterogeneous datasets (individual pricing difficult) might be helpful here.

Third, there is no proper pricing without a solid institutional structure. Pricing requires institution building. Any negotiation requires parties to organize themselves thoroughly, requires them to know who they represent, and requires them to dispose of sufficient expertise on data, pricing and taxing. Negotiations may require middlemen, the "data-agents". Negotiations about pricing require certain rules in terms of who gets to participate and how agreements are forged. In the data-pricing examples mentioned thus far, Jaguar's loyalty programme, the price setting is a one-sided offer provided by the service provider. If price setting is to be the result of negotiations with customer representatives, then institution building is inevitable.

5.4 Challenging the business proposition and, therefore, the business model

Companies such as Facebook and Google harvest data and subsequently use it for their business proposition; here, data is used to profile users, enabling Facebook and Google customers to target users that are of interest to them. These customers may be companies, but also political parties who may target users with political messages tailored to their profiles. Here, the data cost is zero, as profit is being realized with personalized adverts.

Microtargeting and precision-marketing come with great promises. One study about precision-marketing states: 'Marketers need continually refreshed data from a variety of sources and at a far more detailed level—looking as deeply as the city-block level in some cases'.[19] The phrase 'city-block level' sounds very powerful and precise.

19   Bibby, C., Gordon, J., Schuler, G., and Stein, E. (2021). The big reset: Data-driven marketing in the next normal. McKinsey & Company.

Business models: effectiveness and legitimacy

The business models of companies offering precision-marketing are highly dependent on these propositions, and so it is interesting to open the black box of these business propositions. Is user profiling and personalized advertising as effective as the tech giants suggest? How can this effectiveness be proven? Why is there not more more insight into this alleged effectiveness? A discussion about the business proposition touches upon business models and may be of significant impact. The question, therefore, is whether the promise of precision marketing can be fulfilled:

– Has the right target group been identified? An entrepreneur who, for example, sells travel gear, may be interested in the category "frequent travellers". But the question remains as to whether the file of frequent travellers indeed consists of frequent travellers—is the file overly diluted or is there, perhaps, the chance that a large group of travellers are not included? In a research study conducted among Facebook users, a quarter of respondents stated that Facebook classifications do not offer a good representation of them.[20] Also, it is hard to check whether data providers can provide an accurate image of users. Research suggests that they may miss the mark significantly.[21]

– What data is needed to identify this target group? Maybe individualized marketing requires a limited dataset, one that hardly invades privacy? When a limited dataset suffices, the question arises as to why, nevertheless, so much data is still gathered about individual users.

– Do personalized adverts—or does precision marketing—impact the target group? There are doubts about "search

20 Hitlin, P., and Raine, R. (January 16, 2018). *Facebook Algorithms and Personal Data*, Pew Research Center Internet & Technology..

21 Neumann, N., Tucker, C. E., and Whitfield, T. (2019). How Effective is Third-party consumer profiling and audience delivery?: Evidence from field studies. *Marketing Science-Frontiers*, pp. 1–33.

engine marketing", adverts that pop-up next to the search results.[22]

– Research shows that citizens are persuaded by political messages that match their profiles,[23] or that these messages lead to voters being less likely to defect from their party.[24] However, research also shows that microtargeting does not affect the propensity to vote for a candidate,[25] thereby suggesting that the assumption that personalized advertising works is being made to easily.

A lot of this research is still too fragmented, and its outcomes rely heavily on the context. Microtargeting in a polarized two-party system likely has different effects than it does in a consensus-oriented multi-party system. The impact of commercial precision-marketing will depend on the characteristics of a market—what works in one market may not work in another. But this variety only confirms the necessity of opening up the black box of microtargeting or precision-marketing. The more clients know about the impact of precision-marketing, the more informed they can be when deciding whether they want to make use of it. Currently, advertisers often do not know—for reasons of privacy—where their adverts end up. Moreover, Facebook adverts have to meet two criteria; advertisers have to reach their target group (for instance, frequent travellers), but it is in Facebook's interest that the user has a positive experience.

22 Blake, T., Nosko, C., and Tadelis, S. (2015). Consumer Heterogeneity and Paid Search Effectiveness: A Large-Scale Field Experiment. *Econometrica, 83*(1), pp. 155–174.

23 Zarouali, B., Dobber, T., De Pauw, G., and de Vreese, C. (2020). Using a Personality-Profiling Algorithm to Investigate Political Microtargeting: Assessing the Persuasion Effects of Personality-Tailored Ads on Social Media, *Communication Research*, doi: 0093650220961965.

24 Lavigne, M. (2020). *Strengthening ties: The influence of microtargeting on partisan attitudes and the vote*, Party Politics, doi: 10.1177/1354068820918387.

25 Krotzek, L. J. (2019). Inside the voter's mind: the effect of psychometric micro-targeting on feelings toward and propensity to vote for a candidate. *International Journal of Communication, 13*(21), pp. 3609–3629.

These two interests are carefully weighed by Facebook, which does not exactly make the process of personalized advertising more transparent.

The considerations above mainly relate to the effectiveness of personal adverts. These considerations also have a moral component:

– In personalized political adverts, the question arises as to whether the adverts' content is factually correct—or if personalized advertising is being used in order to spread evidentially fake information.
– Political microtargeting can harm the public process of deliberation, a key characteristic of a democracy. Non-targeted voters will not receive certain information and targeted voters' information is kept away from the public eye.[26]
– The black box also means that it is difficult to ascertain whether the GDPR principles for harvesting data are being taken into consideration. When more data is being gathered than strictly necessary for the provision of a particular service (here, personalized advertising), this may be at odds with the principle of data-minimization.

The considerations of effectiveness and morality result in Figure 5.1. If there are moral doubts about precision-marketing, the legitimacy of precision-marketing may be low. The scheme depicts three problematic situations, in quadrants II, III, and IV service is not effective, or it is, but is morally dubious.

Effectiveness and legitimacy may strengthen each other. Clients who have doubts about the legitimacy of using personalized adverts may also become more critical in terms of these adverts' effectiveness—a movement may occur from quadrant II to quadrant IV. The idea here is that opening the black box leads to increased insight for customers (in the case of personalized advertising, companies who buy adverts) and subsequently to

26   Bayer, J. (2020). Double harm to voters: data-driven micro-targeting and democratic public discourse. *Internet Policy Review*, 9(1), pp. 1–17, doi: 10.14763/2020.1.1460.

	Effectiveness high	Effectiveness low
Legitimacy high	I	II
Legitimacy low	III	IV

figure 5.1 *The effectiveness and legitimacy of personalized advertising*

a more critical attitude toward data-gathering for reasons of effectiveness or legitimacy.

In 2020, Unilever decided to refrain from advertising on Facebook, Instagram, and Twitter: 'The complexities of the current cultural landscape have placed a renewed responsibility on brands to learn, respond and act to drive a trusted and safe digital ecosystem (...) Continuing to advertise on these platforms at this time would not add value to people and society.'[27] Companies such as the North Face and Patagonia took similar decisions. Data is being harvested, it is unclear what its effectiveness and legitimacy is, and so advertisers pull back.

Thus far, the examples discussed above mainly focus on precision marketing but, of course, there are many other business propositions. Pornhub is a platform that offers users access to pornographic videos to the website's visitors, including many amateur videos. Many videos are "non-verified", some of them consist of rape and revenge porn. A number of journalists requested that more attention be given to this phenomenon.[28] Consequently, the black box of the website was cracked open: much the website's material turned out to be non-consensual. The legitimacy of this is, of course, zero. This situation did not lead to immediate purging of the website, but this changed when when two credit card companies decided to no longer facilitate Pornhub payments—obviously, this is a strong incentive for the website to clean up its video files and to delete non-consensual

27   Kelly, M. (June 26, 2020). *Unilever will pull ads from Facebook, Instagram, and Twitter for the rest of the year*, The Verge.
28   Kristof, N. (December 4, 2020). *The Children of Pornhub*, The New York Times.

content.[29] Opening the black box shows that data and information legitimacy is problematic and subsequently leads to action, not by users in this case, but by the parties facilitating payments.

What roles can government play?

From a governance perspective, it may be quite appealing to open up the black box of the business proposition—to analyse whether the promise of personalized advertising is fulfilled and whether the gathering of data is legitimate. Governments may implement a multitude of measures, contributing to the opening up of the black box. Here are a few examples.

An interesting tool is the publication of ads used for political microtargeting in publicly accessible libraries. The idea is mainly inspired by worries about the quality of public debate. Through microtargeting, certain party messages are hidden from the public eye. When all ads are to be registered in a central database, this enables third parties to analyse these ads and to identify malicious advertisers.[30] This is not only beneficial to a healthy public debate, but a database is also a way of making the business model for those who sell political ads more transparent. Visibility and a public debate about the micro-targeted messages may have an impact on their effectiveness.

The right of access to personal data can also contribute to opening the black box of business models. This right gives users an insight into what data companies have and apparently need for their business models. It might be a highly unpleasant surprise for users to learn what data companies have,[31] and the next step may be to challenge them accordingly: Why do they

29   Alger, S. (December 26, 2020). *The Freakout Over Pornhub's Mass Deletion*. The Pink.

30   Edelson, L., Lauinger, T., and McCoy, D. (2020). A Security Analysis of the Facebook Ad Library, *2020 IEEE Symposium on Security and Privacy*, pp. 661–678, doi: 10.1109/SP40000.2020.00084.

31   Hill, K. (November 5, 2019). *I Got Access to My Secret Consumer Score. Now You Can Get Yours, Too*, The New York Times.

need this data, how does this data contribute to the business proposition?

Another example of opening the black box concerns explaining why personalized adverts are offered: 'This ad thinks...

- ...you're male, actively consolidating your debt and are a high spender at luxury department stores,
- ... you're a cybersecurity expert, female and go to art events in the desert,
- ... you're trying to lose weight but still love bakeries'.[32]

The origin of the information can also be indicated (e.g., search behaviour, credit card information). When this happens on a grand scale it may become clear whether the profiles are often wrong or which sources reveal the most information. Perhaps, as a consequence of this, users will become more alert in terms of handing over data. In the event that the profiles are terribly precise, this may also make users more alert. The cybersecurity expert, who recently went to Burning Man, perhaps does not want everyone to know that she attended the event.

Developments such as these emerge in the market, and at the initiative of journalists, tech companies, advocacy groups, et cetera. The role of government can be to monitor these developments and, if they prove to be effective, to impose these practices as an obligation to companies.

And then there is the option of a government simply prohibiting personalized advertising. In 2020, the European Parliament supported a proposition to prohibit personalized advertising.[33] In 2021, Google announced that it will phase out third-party cookies, resulting in targeted advertising being less based on

---

32 Thompson, S. A. (April 30, 2019). *These Ads Think They Know You*, The New York Times.

33 Parliament 'calls on the Commission to ban platforms from displaying micro-targeted advertisements', European Parliament resolution of 18 June 2020 on competition policy: doi: www.europarl.europa.eu/doceo/document/ TA-9-2020-0158_EN.html.

individual data.[34] Possibly, there is no direct relation with the threat from the European Parliament, but an important argument for Google is the fact that privacy concerns are increasingly present, and, moreover, that privacy enhancing technologies are available, thereby facilitating this step. Call this the shadow of the law: the threat that personalized advertising may be regulated in one way or another is an incentive to search for precision-marketing that is less dependent upon individual user data.

5.5   Creating barriers in the data-journey—breaking up companies

Data travels, which may ultimately result in privacy being violated. As mentioned above, governance may entail the creation of a number of barriers during this journey, barrier models that can be found in the literature on large-scale, man-made disasters. The disaster often occurs through a process of technical and human failures. Analysts can think such a process through, to find out what the most vulnerable activities are in this process, by creating an "event-tree analysis". Subsequently, a number of barriers can be designed that serve as a safety-valve, these barriers may be technological, organizational, or procedural. Again, the central idea here is redundancy: when there are sufficient barriers in place, and one or more of them do not work, there still are barriers that remain to prevent the disaster. Barriers may be focused on prevention of the disaster or on protection against its consequences.[35] When this is translated into data and privacy, we see that during the data-journey, data can be faced with barriers that prevent the continuation of the journey or that only allow continuation if certain conditions are met. In

34   Temkin, D. (March 3, 2021). Charting a course towards a more privacy-first web, Google Ads & Commerce Blog.
35   Hollnagel, E. (1999). Accident Analysis and Barrier Functions, IFE, pp. 1–34.

this chapter about market mechanisms, I discuss this strategy, because breaking up economic activities is an important tool in the economic toolbox.[36]

Barriers during the data-journey/in the data stream

Regulators increasingly create more barriers during the data-journey (or in the data stream), both between and within companies.

Limiting data-transactions between companies. Here, the GDPR principle of purpose and storage limitation comes to mind, which may disturb the data-journey. Another example is an "adequacy decision" by the European Commission. If a third country offers an adequate level of data-protection, data can be more easily transferred to companies in this country than without such an adequacy decision. Without such a decision, there are extra safeguards for data transfers—or, put differently, there are more barriers during the data-journey.

Limiting data-accumulation within companies. Where tech giants are concerned, the exchange of data often takes place within the walls of the company. In 2019, the German Bundeskartelamt took a number of decisions to counter data-accumulation within Facebook. WhatsApp and Instagram are owned by Facebook, but the German regulator stated that 'assigning the data to Facebook user accounts will only be possible subject to the users' voluntary consent. Where consent is not given, the data must remain with the respective service and cannot be processed in combination with Facebook data'.[37] Although it

36   Cave, M. (2006). Six Degrees of Separation Operation: Separation as a Remedy in European Telecommunications Regulation, *Communications and Strategies*, pp. 1–15.
37   Although Facebook appealed during the writing of this book, it is clear that possibilities present themselves here nonetheless.

is not quite clear whether the point of view of the Competition Authority will stand,[38] it is clear that internal unbundling may be an important instrument in creating barriers within the data-journey.

The prospect that national regulators may undertake a host of actions to do this may already be an incentive for the companies in question to be hesitant in terms of data accumulation. Companies may also implement their own measures. Facebook can allow app developers access to Facebook data. This access runs through an API (Application Programming Interface). Influenced by public critique on Facebook, the company removed APIs and has denied many applications access to APIs. This "blacklisting" is, again, a barrier within the data-journey.

Limiting the collection and use of data due to distortion of competition. More generally, regulators are using competition regulation to limit the power of companies like Facebook—the decision by the German Bundeskartelamt is one example. EU Commissioner Margrethe Vestager explains the use of competition law, following an investigation into Facebook:

'Facebook collects vast troves of data on the activities of users of its social network and beyond, enabling it to target specific customer groups. We will look in detail at whether this data gives Facebook an undue competitive advantage in particular on the online classified ads sector, where people buy and sell goods every day, and where Facebook also competes with companies from which it collects data. In today's digital economy, data should not be used in ways that distort competition.'[39]

Although competition regulation can contribute to data protection, this is not always the case. If a tech giant has a platform

38 Stolton, S. (2021). *German legal dispute over Facebook data use sent to European Court of Justice.* Euractiv, https://www.euractiv.com/section/data-protection/news/german-legal-dispute-over-facebook-data-use-sent-to-european-court-of-justice/.

39 https://ec.europa.eu/commission/presscorner/detail/en/ip_21_2848.

and offers services on this platform there might be a competition issue: the tech giant can regulate the entry of its competitors and create a competitive advantage for its own services. Many tech giants defend these entry rules with the argument that they need to safeguard privacy and have to limit competition for privacy reasons.

Data portability. The idea of data portability—"service-switching" or "multi-homing"—may also be seen as a tool to add barriers to the data-journey. Users are often the service provider's captive, leaving a provider may result in loss of valuable data, from very personal data (e.g., pictures or someone's running data), to data with a high economic value (e.g., companies that have built years of reviews or scores). When users are the captives or providers this is not only damaging to competition and innovation, it also means that an accumulation of data occurs with a platform or service provider.

Article 20 of the GDPR gives 'data subjects' the right to data portability: the right to receive all data that a company has in a structured and legible fashion, and to transfer this data from one company to the other. Data portability can be framed as a strategy to create barriers within the data-journey. According to the data-journey metaphor, data travels along various stations (the companies who possess and use the data). Data portability means that this data is transported from company A to company B, and that station A no longer lies on the route of the data-journey. Disconnecting station A from the data-journey may be conducive to privacy; for example, if station B offers a more privacy-friendly proposition. Station A may anticipate the data transfer by investing more in privacy and making it unattractive to leave A.

Data-portability is, of course, more complicated in practice than it is on paper—services are tied to other services or particular hardware. Moreover, data-portability may also have perverse effects: data might be transferred to a provider who is less precise in terms of privacy, or data that has been gathered through privacy violations may resume its travels elsewhere.[40] Data portability may lead to more data being transferred to the tech giants, who can thus strengthen their dominance.[41] But the concept does its work, companies invest in making data transferable and, here too, a tipping point may occur; the more data-portability is being offered as a service, the more obvious this becomes for users, and the more they will demand this service.

Breaking up companies

A follow-up to cutting the data-journey may be achieved by breaking up companies that possess vast amounts of data. The tech giants have the advantage of network effects—the more users a social network has, the more attractive it becomes for others to also become a user of the network. Through these network effects, a winner-takes-all market may occur, with various negative implications for companies looking to enter that market.

These economic deliberations are, of course, relevant in terms of privacy. An enormous accumulation of data may happen with the tech giants and, furthermore, they can simply buy other companies with their data (Facebook, for example, has acquired WhatsApp and Instagram). All this may lead to a monopolistic situation, with the risk of abusing market power. The remedy can be the break-up of these companies. The argument is primarily economic in nature:

- Market power is at the expense of competition and innovation. The consequences can be far reaching, right up to the early phases of innovation processes. Foroohar points to

40   See the warnings in, Digital Competition Expert Panel. (2019). *Unlocking digital competition*, London: HM Treasury.
41   Borgogno, O., and Colangelo, G. (2019). Data sharing and interoperability: Fostering innovation and competition through APIs. *Computer Law & Security Review, 35*(5), p. 105314. https://doi.org/10.1016/j.clsr.2019.03.008.

banks being less prone to provide competitors of incumbents with credit, where companies with intangible assets are already less attractive creditors, and this is even truer when they enter a winner-takes-all market.[42]
–   Moreover, key players accumulate such a gigantic amount of money, that this in itself may be threatening to the stability of the financial system or the economy as a whole, such as certain banks that, during the financial crisis of 2007–2008, were "too big to fail".

Data: the accumulation versus transaction dilemma

Breaking up is too vast a subject to address on a few pages. Here, I will focus only on the question that concerns the effect that the break-up of big companies may have on data protection and privacy protection, and shall present a narrative in three steps, which may be helpful in comprehending the relation between breaking up and privacy.

Step one: the market of data-gathering, -storage, and -usage is not solely comprised by big tech-companies. There are of course many other companies that provide services through the Internet and harvest data—from cars to the booking sites, from credit cards to route planners. There is data exchange between services and between apps, for example. There are countless data-brokers: companies who gather and analyse data, and who buy and sell data files. To sum up, there is an arcane web of transactions, in which data is continually generated, collected, enriched, and exchanged. These transactions take place everywhere. Consider just one example: China develops an AI platform City Brain, through which data on processes and individuals within a city is being gathered and used. These systems are being sold to cities that take out loans from Chinese banks. Part of the conditions—or of refinancing conditions—may be that China is given access to the data of these

42   Foroohar, R. (2019). *Don't Be Evil: The Case Against Big Tech*, Australia: Currency Press.

systems.[43] Data is gathered and exchanged within a global web of cities, actors within these cities, banks, and Chinese institutions.

This means that, from the perspective of privacy, there are two realities, which I will name "accumulation" and "transaction":

– First, the accumulation of data in one, powerful hand. This is the current situation regarding tech giants: an enormous accumulation of data in one hand. Each of these tech-giants disposes of obscure mountains of data. Connecting data that is part of these data mountains may lead to serious privacy violations. The data mountains are continuously growing because of network effects.

– Second, data transactions within an arcane web of many hands. Countless data transactions exist, passing through many hands within an equally opaque, spaghetti-like web of data transfers. Pairings between data that are part of these transactions may lead to serious privacy violations. The spaghetti-web is ever expanding.

Step two: a thought experiment. Breaking up companies may mean the disappearance of a tech giant and will lead to a multi-plication of companies that will conduct data transactions among themselves. This move from the world of accumulation to the world of transaction does not necessarily result in more privacy protection. When both accumulation and transaction can lead to privacy violations, then the choice as to whether to break up or not break up becomes less clear and more of a dilemma, one that is summarized in Figure 5.2.[44]

The advantage of the many hands (Figure 5.2, quadrant II) is that data is spread over many more players. This means that it is less simple to connect data since this requires a transaction, and transactions imply a variety of costs.

43 Anderson, R. (September 15, 2020). The Panopticon is Already Here. *The Atlantic.* https://www.theatlantic.com/magazine/archive/2020/09/china-ai-surveillance/614197/

44 Inspired by Johnson, B. (1996). *Polarity Management,* Amhurst: HRD Press.

	Accumulation - One hand	Transaction - Many hands
Pro	I One responsible party, who can be held accountable for all privacy breaches	II Data spread over a great number of players, so less possibilities to connect the dots
Con	III Accumulation of data, which leads to an obscure data-mountain, and thus is a breeding ground for privacy breaches	IV Arcane spaghetti-like network of data-transactions, for which nobody is responsible

figure 5.2 *Pros and cons of accumulation or transactions of data*

The disadvantage of one hand (Figure 5.2, quadrant III) concerns the accumulation of data—tech-giants dispose of continually expanding data mountains. However, one hand also has an advantage (quadrant I). When data is in one hand, there is a clear responsibility regarding the misuse of data. Furthermore, big companies may be held to a higher standard in terms of the measures they take because they have more expertise and more resources.

If data is in many hands, responsibility might become a diffuse affair (Figure 5.2, quadrant IV). The more data exchange through transactions, the less clear it might be as to who should be held responsible for the misuse of data, or, at least, the higher the cost of finding out who is responsible for this misuse.

It is a difficult dilemma. One may think of the fight against hate speech and fake news. When the spreading of hate speech and fake news is concentrated in the hands of one tech giant, this party can be held accountable, and giants can, on account of their size, implement extensive measures. When spreading fake news and hate speech runs via a vast number of parties, government control might become increasingly more difficult, or even develop into a whack-a-mole-like process.

On the other hand, a person who spreads fake news through the platform of a tech giant potentially has greater impact—and so this person also profits from network effects. The question is then concerned with what is worse, fake news being spread through the platform of a tech giant, which is potentially quite impactful, but which is also subject to the tech giant's tools to combat fake news, or, alternatively, fake news being spread through a web of smaller players, which is potentially less impactful but that maybe also be also harder to fight?

Moreover, not only the dilemma exists, we also do not know what the consequences of breaking up will be. If tech giants disappear and more midsize players appear, it is, currently, hard to predict what strategies they will develop and what the impact will be on phenomena such as fake news and hate speech. Perhaps these midsize players will present the best of both worlds—less misuse of data but still clear responsibilities—or, perhaps, the worst.

Note that this observation does not diminish the economic arguments for the breaking up of these companies, but these economic arguments are not necessarily in line with privacy related arguments.

Step three. When a dilemma exists, and nobody knows exactly what the new reality will be, the appropriate strategy then becomes one of incremental decision making. This means that breaking up or not breaking up is not a "big bang" decision but rather a series of small steps. Incremental decision-making makes it possible to learn and to improve the breaking-up strategy. One may think of the following steps:

- prohibiting certain types of personalized adverts in order to diminish the chance of online manipulation;
- commanding platforms to allow competitors on the platforms to create a level playing-field, thereby denying platforms the right to favour their own services;[45]
- prohibiting the acquisition of companies, in particular, new, innovative companies;

45   Khan, L. M. (2017). Amazon's Anti-Trust Paradox. *The Yale Law Journal*, 126(3), pp. 717–722.

- the obligation to implement certain internal divisions;
- the establishing of sector-specific competition authorities in addition to a general watchdog.[46]

In an incremental process, governments may learn what the impact of such measures will be. Do they diminish market power? Do they lead to more or less protection of privacy? Are follow-up actions necessary? Privacy is a process but breaking up is also a process.

5.6   The power of the market and resilience

This chapter has addressed market mechanisms, which may be beneficial for more privacy protection. How do these market mechanisms contribute to resilient governance?

The first answer to this question is, again, that several mechanisms result in downstream interventions, not only in upstream interventions. Opening the black box is a downstream intervention. Upstream, companies collect and process data to develop a business proposition, for example, the service of personalized advertising. Downstream, their potential clients might consider that using these services and opening the black box might impact the decision they make. If they learn that the business proposition depends on large-scale data collection, they might decide to pull back (take the example of Unilever, discussed earlier) because of privacy concerns, which might be an incentive for less upstream data-gathering.

Taxing and the forming of funds is also a downstream intervention. Data is collected upstream and used downstream, which leads to collective income, something that can be used to invest

46   Digital Competition Expert Panel. (2019). *Unlocking digital competition*, London: HM Treasury; Lohr, S. (October 22, 2020). *Forget Antitrust Laws. To Limit Tech, Some Say a New Regulator Is Needed*, The New York Times.

in, for example, privacy-enhancing technologies.[47] Of course, resilient governance cannot be effective without upstream interventions. Almost all strategies discussed in this chapter would not have emerged, or will not emerge, without ex ante regulation that recognizes citizens' right to privacy.

The second answer is that we encounter resilience according to a second meaning: resilience as redundancy. At a systems level, market mechanisms can create incentives for privacy protection and barriers for privacy breaches. The more market mechanisms are activated, the more incentives and barriers there will be, which eventually result in a redundant system of incentives and barriers. The strength of redundancy is that there are fallback barriers if one of the barriers fails.

The question is, of course, whether a market-based system is sufficiently redundant. The answer is, probably, that it is not, but that market mechanisms at least contribute to redundancy.

The third answer to the question is that, as stated in Chapter 3, resilience can result in restoring the old situation (restoration of violated privacy) or finding a new balance between privacy and other values. In this chapter, we found both types of resilience. Remember the example of the lifestyle insurance—the pricing of data is not only an incentive to give away data, it might also result in a new equilibrium between privacy protection and other values.

Of course, resilient governance cannot be effective without upstream interventions. Almost all strategies discussed in this chapter would not have emerged, or will not emerge, without ex ante regulation that recognizes citizens' right to privacy. Some strategies will have an impact downstream; taxing means that data has been collected and, subsequently, taxed. But taxing might also be defined as an upstream incentive to refrain from

---

47 Depending on the context, taxing might also be defined as an upstream incentive to refrain from harvesting data. Competition for privacy can also be both an upstream and a downstream intervention, depending on the service to which the competition relates (e.g., the ISP, the browser, the search machine).

harvesting data. Competition for privacy can also be both an upstream and a downstream intervention, depending on the service to which the competition relates (e.g., ISP, the browser, the search engine).

Governments can use the power of the state and the power of the market to protect citizens' privacy. There is a third resource of power: society—the topic of the next chapter.

6   The Power of Society

6.1   Introduction

The previous chapters focused on state- and market-based approaches to protecting privacy. In this chapter, I shift the perspective to society—to the empowerment of citizens, communities, or society as a whole. Again, the key concept is resilience. Empowering society means that users acquire the knowledge and competencies to prevent privacy breaches to the fullest extent. When they are more privacy-aware, more privacy-literate, and more data-savvy, users can fulfil an active role in the protection of privacy. Again, resilience has an upstream component (users are empowered early in the data-journey), and a downstream component (users are empowered later in the data-journey).

6.2   Empowerment upstream

There are, of course, many tools to empower users upstream. Relatively simple measures, such as leaving less data, using a variety of passwords, using a VPN connection, or using a privacy-friendly search browser, can contribute to the protection of users' privacy.

The paradox of privacy conditions

In this section I will focus on the use of privacy conditions. Service providers have an obligation to make their privacy conditions explicit, these conditions have to be in line with regulations such those of the the GDPR, and users are able to choose whether they agree to the privacy conditions or not. Theoretically, these privacy conditions empower users but, in practice, this is not always the case. The use of these privacy conditions is a good example of the many strategies service providers use to prevent users from being in control over their own data.

Research shows that users often agree outright with privacy conditions. How may this behaviour be explained, and what can we learn from it?

The explanation begins with privacy requiring a trade-off with other values: health, access to information, safety, user convenience. This trade-off is complicated by a variety of other factors, including users' sense of urgency—does the user need the information urgently or not? The fact that other values need to be weighed and that there is often a high sense of urgency may be exploited by service-providers in four, roughly distinct ways.

–   Firstly, there often is a "take-it-or-leave-it" offer. Here, users can choose between agreeing with the provider's privacy conditions, or having limited or non-existent access their services.[1] This means that a user (1) is faced with an either/or offer (2) in an ambiguous context (3) that requires a complicated trade off. It does not take a lot of imagination to grasp the consequences of this choice—many users will agree to the privacy conditions. The benefits of agreeing are clear, and the costs are highly diffuse and will only occur in the long term.[2]

–   Secondly, the decision to accept the privacy conditions always needs to be made 'in the actual moment'.[3] Imagine that a person searches for information about a particular medical condition and has to consider the need for information on the one hand and privacy on the other. This trade-off must be made at the precise moment at which the person wants to have this information. The outcome is obvious—privacy loses out.

–   Thirdly, there is the framing of the privacy conditions themselves. These can be formulated in such a way that the

1   Santario, A. (May 6, 2018). *What the GDPR, Europe's Tough New Data Law, Means for You*, The New York Times.

2   Acquisti, A., and Grossklags, J. (2005). Privacy and Rationality in Individual Decision Making. *IEEE Security & Privacy, 3*(1), pp. 26–33.

3   Barth, S., and De Jong, M. D. (2017). The privacy paradox: Investigating discrepancies between expressed privacy concerns and actual online behavior—A systematic literature review. *Telematics and informatics, 34*(7), pp. 1038–1058.

option of stricter privacy seems less attractive, or even less ethically responsible. The Norwegian Consumers' Authority mentions the framing of facial recognition technology by certain companies as an example. Primarily, these companies indicate what the technology's function is, '[it] helps protect you from strangers using your photo' and 'tells people with visual impairments who's in a photo or video'. Subsequently, the consequences of turning facial recognition off are indicated: 'if you keep face recognition turned off, we won't be able to use this technology if a stranger uses your photo to impersonate you. If someone uses a screen reader, they won't be told when you're in a photo unless you're tagged'.[4] Clearly, this framing nudges the user towards turning on this option—in such a way that it almost seems unethical to disagree to facial recognition.

– Fourthly, there is a host of additional nudges. For example, the length of the privacy conditions themselves, as reading them requires a lot of time, which is disproportionate to the time needed to search for the right information.[5] Alternatively, one may think of the use of pop-up screens. The privacy conditions appear as a pop-up in front of the relevant webpage and block the site the user wants to visit. The natural tendency of many users is to click away pop-up screens, something that can only be achieved by agreeing to the privacy conditions they stipulate. If the privacy conditions were to appear as a customary page, this nudge would not be present.[6] What is also important is that privacy conditions are written for everyone, and the associated risk is well-known. For those who know a lot about privacy, they may be too general in nature, but for those who are not very familiar

4   Forbrukerrådet. (2018). *Deceived by design, How tech companies use dark patterns to discourage us from exercising our rights to privacy*, Oslo: Forbrukerrådet (p. 22).
5   Editorial Bord New York Times. (February 2, 2019). How Silicon Valley Puts the 'Con' in Consent, The New York Times.
6   Chen, B. X. (May 23, 2018). *Getting a Flood of GDPR-Related Privacy Policy Updates? Read Them*, The New York Times.

with privacy, they may be overly detailed. Again, this acts as a nudge because, when something can be said to have been "written for everyone", it is likely that it has, in fact, been written for no one—something that a user may swiftly overlook.

These four mechanisms may or may not be intentionally used by service providers. When mechanisms such as these are used with intent, we speak of "strategic behaviour" or "dark patterns". Strategic behaviour is when the provider plays a game with the users and continually exploits one or more of these mechanisms. Dark patterns are 'tricks used in websites and apps that make you buy or sign up for things that you didn't mean to'.[7]

All this leads to a remarkable paradox. Privacy conditions should serve as a tool to empower users: providers are forced to be transparent about their privacy conditions and it is up to the user accept or reject them. However, because of the four aforementioned mechanisms, there is a strong incentive for users to dismiss opting for the possibility to decline the privacy conditions—and consequently the power of the provider increases. Users agree with the conditions that companies impose on them, thereby realizing the paradox: privacy conditions should empower users but, instead, service providers use them to obtain more power.[8]

There are many available strategies for dismantling this:
– The "take it or leave it" dichotomy can be eliminated by allowing greater variety of choice—"granular preferences". For example, users can indicate, when using an app, which information is or is not to be used by the service provider, or they can state in the app which access to other apps they

7   www.darkpatterns.org.
8   Moreover, the more services a company offers, the easier it is for these companies to nudge users into consenting. Goldfarb, A., and Tucker, C. (2012). Privacy and innovation. *Innovation Policy and the Economy*, 12(1), pp. 65–90, doi: 10.1086/663156.

allow.[9] In addition, it may help if users obtain an insight into the degree to which they, in turn, give third parties insights into their data. When particular tools inform users that they are entrusting third parties with a tremendous amount of private information, this may influence their views on privacy and their behaviour.

– When the analysis reveals that privacy conditions have been written for everyone—and, ultimately, for no-one—the solution may be that differentiation is necessary. Information about privacy conditions can be adjusted to users' expertise. There are novices and experts, near-experts, and selective sharers. A person who has never looked at their privacy settings should receive more basic information than those people who continuously enhance their privacy settings.[10]

– Users are required to decide in the moment but, of course, this decision can be reversed. Monitoring apps are available—apps that analyse the privacy conditions of all the user's apps and, as such, offer insights into the labyrinth of user choices. These apps also offer the user the possibility to reverse such choices. When a service provider demands the sharing of particular data (location, directories, phone number), there are apps that support users by providing fake data, thereby maintaining the provision of service.

Measures such as these may fortify the users' position, though there are and will be alternative strategies; invariably, three important comments must be made, comments that are relevant to both these and other strategies are as follows:

9   Alpers, S., Betz, S., Fritsch, A., Oberweis, A., Schiefer, G., and Wagner, M. (2018). Citizen Empowerment by a Technical Approach for Privacy Enforcement. In, *Proceedings of the 8th International Conference on Cloud Computing and Services Science* (Vol. 1), CLOSER, pp. 589–595.

10 Wisniewski, P. J., Knijnenburg, B. P., and Lipford, H. R. (2017). Making privacy personal: Profiling social network users to inform privacy education and nudging. *International Journal of Human-Computer Studies, 98,* pp. 95–108.

One: the strategies are and will remain part of a cat-and-mouse game. The service provider may present a variety of options to the user but, simultaneously, incorporate incentives that make them opt for making their data available in virtually all cases. A service provider may decide to align the explanation of privacy conditions to the level of different types of users, from novices to experts. However, this may in turn lead to an expanding body of rules. Differentiating between types of users can help, however, it may require data and profiling to determine someone's level of expertise. There still might be a mismatch between the user's knowledge and the wording of the privacy conditions presented to them— all these "howevers" can be exploited in the cat-and-mouse game.

Two: users have an ambiguous attitude—they need to make a trade-off between privacy and other values, a situation that is not going to change. An ambiguous user who is presented with a "take it or leave it proposition" will, by and large, accept privacy conditions. A person who is offered a variety of options may still show the same behaviour or make a random choice since the revenues of accepting are clear and the cost is diffuse. Moreover, variety means that a user needs to consider options available to them, which entails transaction costs because it requires time for the user to make their decision; therefore, accepting the easiest option seems attractive.

Three: behind many strategies, there are assumptions about users, which are questionable.

– The assumption that a user is not just privacy-aware, but also prepared to put this awareness to action. Research shows that there is more nuance to this—several authors refer to a privacy-paradox here: users are worried about their privacy, but they do not act accordingly.[11] There is an important dif-

---

11   Pierson J. (2015) Privacy and Empowerment in Connective Media. In: Tiropanis T., Vakali A., Sartori L., Burnap P. (eds) Internet Science. INSCI 2015. *Lecture Notes in Computer Science,* vol 9089. Springer, Cham. https://doi.org/10.1007/978-3-319-18609-2_1; Barth, S., and De Jong, M. D. (2017). The privacy paradox: Investigating discrepancies between expressed privacy concerns and actual online behavior—A systematic literature review. *Telematics and informatics, 34*(7), pp. 1038–1058.

ference between their "stated" and "revealed" preferences—a classic concept in literature about consumer behaviour.[12]

- The assumption that users will take the time to weigh their options and to protect their privacy—while in actuality, they are required to decide in the actual moment.
- The assumption that they are sufficiently tech-savvy to protect their privacy. This is not always the case, put mildly—while technical familiarity and Internet skills are an important predictor when it comes to actions to protect personal data.[13]

In addition, users are continuously confronted with privacy conditions and are also continuously required to make choices, that, again, are not conducive to privacy protection. The many different choices about different privacy conditions invoke the image of a colander; consider a colander filled with data, you may try to close every hole in the colander through the use of privacy conditions but you will never fully succeed in trapping it all inside.

Privacy conditions and the strategy of contextualization

So, under a somewhat grimmer outlook—what does all this entail in terms of the central question in this chapter, and how can user empowerment contribute to the upstream protection of privacy?

One: privacy conditions do, of course, matter. Without these conditions, significantly less safeguarding of user privacy would exist. Privacy protection is a cat-and-mouse game, and it may be functional to simply continue this game by continuously working towards better and more effective privacy conditions. The measures described above give service providers a harder time

12   Samuelson, P. A. (1948). Consumption Theory in Terms of Revealed Preference. *Economica, New Series*, 15(60), pp. 243–253.
13   Büchi, M., Just, N., and Latzer, M. (2017). Caring is not enough: the importance of Internet skills for online privacy protection. *Information, Communication & Society*, 20(8), pp. 1261–1278.

when harvesting data. Granulation, prohibiting dark patterns, the obligation to use simple language—all may contribute to the realization of more accessible privacy conditions that users would sooner and more readily utilize.

Two: what is equally important is the strategy of contextualization, consider the famous quote of the French author Antoine de Saint-Exupéry:

> If you want to build a ship,
> don't drum up people to collect wood.
> don't assign them tasks and work,
> but rather teach them to long
> for the endless immensity of the sea.

This quote is widely used and is, therefore, somewhat frayed, but it nevertheless offers an important insight. The manual on "how to build a ship" will only come to life when there is a longing for the sea. The person who longs for the sea becomes interested in the question of how one builds a ship and is prepared to master this skill. The analogy is clear: privacy conditions and other measures that are focused on upstream empowerment and will only come to life for a user when there is a longing for privacy—hence the concept of contextualization.

How can this context be created? How can this longing be cultivated?

- Through governments and companies' continuously making explicit what the damage of privacy violations may be. Campaigns that warn users about data sharing possibly have the most harmful consequences. For example, the construction of a digital identity that does not correspond to a person's true identity may make users more alert in terms of data sharing.
- Generally speaking, when it is visible to users what the perverse impact of handing over data will be, this may generate an incentive to be more alert when doing so. Consider the following short thought experiment. A user shares the PIN of a bank account and is subsequently confronted with financial

	Weak negative impact	Strong negative impact
Indirect relation with data sharing	I	II
Direct relation with data sharing	III	IV
		PIN-code Personalised fishing mails Doxing

figure 6.1 Conditions within which users are more or less alert to privacy

fraud—a large sum is being transferred from their account. It is likely that this experience will be a strong incentive to be more cautious in the future. Why? Because there is a negative effect (loss of money) and a direct relation between handing over the data (the PIN-code) and these negative effects. The thought experiment makes it clear what the key message in communication campaigns about privacy should be, namely, that data-sharing may result in direct harm (see quadrant IV in Figure 6.1). Many users will think that quadrant I in Figure 6.1 represents reality; they share data, which will sometimes have a negative impact, but this impact is weak and only indirectly related to the data they have shared. However, there are also many situations represented by quadrant IV in Figure 6.1. Due to data sharing, users may become an easy victim of phishing mails (since they are more personalized) or doxing. The more users who understand that quadrant IV situations are a real threat, the more interested they may become in protecting their privacy. The examples in quadrants I–III will probably capture their imagination to a lesser extent and, therefore, these are less impactful in terms of leading their attention towards privacy.

- Privacy can be ensured more appealing when other, more attractive values are included. Think of the use of a VPN connection; this is not just beneficial to privacy, it also makes a user less vulnerable to internet fraudsters and offers access to foreign websites that are blocked via a regular connection.

- If there is sea, there is land, and a longing for the sea can be fuelled by an aversion to the land. For example, the ruling of the Norwegian Consumers Authority to which I previously referred, which makes visible how cunning companies are when it comes to framing privacy conditions and giving nudges. Additionally, an insight into tech-giants' dark patterns can be a breeding ground for a longing for privacy. Amazon Prime, for instance, makes unsubscribing very difficult—a link to do this is placed in a highly illogical section of the website.[14] Making this particular behaviour visible through naming and shaming may have two advantages: the longing for privacy in users increases, and certain providers may be sensitive to naming and shaming and, therefore, change their behaviour.

Three: one may guess the third answer. When empowerment upstream reaches its natural boundaries, it becomes important to also invest in empowerment downstream. Privacy violation is a process, after all, which does not end when data and information have been handed over to third parties.

6.3   Patterns: locking-in and locking-out

Data ends up in the hands of third parties, who may use data to cause privacy violations of types 1–4. The concept of downstream empowerment implies that:
- Users understand the perverse effects of privacy violations of types 1–4, not just the four violations individually, but also the patterns they lead to collectively. In this chapter, I call these patterns (1) locking-in and (2) locking-out.
- Users know how to weaponize themselves against these perverse effects and patterns of locking-in and locking-out.

14   Alonzo, I. (January 14, 2021). *Amazon Prime 'Dark Pattern' of Service Cancellation Explained: Why Consumer Groups Think It's Unfair and Deceptive*, Tech Times.

Patterns: locking-in

The first pattern is locking-in, whereby users hand over data, are profiled with this data, and are subsequently nudged in a particular direction—and may ultimately become locked-in. When this happens it does so as part of a process that is often fairly innocent within a commercial environment, but this becomes significantly less innocent in the world of ideas.

Lock-in in the world of commercial services

In a commercial environment, the process of locking-in entails three waves, which practically every user will recognize.

- Inform. Users who buy their products or services with commercial providers may be alerted to products or services that are in line with their preferences: "customers who viewed this item also viewed", "you may also like", "trending now". Recommendations may be based on a limited dataset (the user's purchasing behaviour), or on a broader dataset—the user's personal profile.
- Influence. Informing may seamlessly transition into influencing. "You may also like" is, perhaps, already a nudge to buy the next product. But there are countless other nudges and incentives to influence our purchasing behaviour, such as "only one room left", "prices will go up in the coming days", "perks" for those who use a particular app, and personalized offers.
- Isolate. The sum of the nudges and incentives may lead to a provider becoming a "preferred supplier"—a user will always go to the same provider for certain products or services. The user then becomes the "captive" of the provider and becomes isolated from other providers. The service provision is up to par, and quick (address and credit card info is already known by the provider) discounts are given for the next purchase, the provider presents a broad array of goods and services, et cetera.

As said above, these mechanisms are often fairly innocent in the world of commercial services, although this may not always be the case (lock-in mechanisms, used on a large scale, can result in monopoly-like situations and lack of competition).

From commercial services to ideas: socio-technical factors leading to lock-in

The three I's (Inform, Influence, Isolate) can have a completely different impact in the world of ideas. The first wave is "Inform", users who show an interest in a particular subject may also be alerted to other information about the same topic: "related news" and "related stories".

In the second wave, "Influence", there is a big difference between the world of commercial products and services on the one hand and that of ideas on the other.

Platforms can earn money by capturing our attention. The more attention, the more interest advertisers have and the more income a platform can generate. How can a platform maintain its grip on our attention? How can it increase the amount of clicks and the time that we spend on it? What impact does that have in the world of ideas? These questions have an answer in five steps.

Step one: values and preconceptions as a system of navigation in the Internet ocean. Through the Internet, we dispose of an ocean of information about societal problems and solutions. How do users handle all this information? What is their navigation system within the ocean of information?

Sometimes users are highly analytical—they absorb information and are interested in a variety of perspectives and lenses. A person who has a particular medical condition will often be open to a host of information concerning diagnoses and treatments, but also for alternative diagnoses and treatments or for second opinions.

But there is also another navigation system, one that is mainly used in the world of ideas. With selecting and interpreting information, users are led by their values—their deepest convictions about what is right or wrong. When someone is, based on their own values, convinced that the neoliberal ideology of privatization and competition is morally good, then this person will naturally be sensitive to information supporting this conviction. Does research prove that competition and privatization have a positive impact on the quality of medical care? This information will probably be accepted—it is in line with someone's values. Does research prove that competition and privatization have a very negative influence on the quality of medical care? There is a good chance that this information is perceived in a more critical manner.

Thanks to the Internet, the ocean of information is always available. This has two consequences:

- The more information users need to process, the more users depend and fall back on their navigation system—their own values and preconceptions.
- The more information, the easier it will be for users to find information that is in line with and supports their values.

Again, there is a paradox here: the more information, the simpler it will be is for us to confirm our own values and preconceptions.

Locking-in is further strengthened because users who select and interpret information from their personal values and biases tend to be forgiving towards fake information.

To illustrate the latter, consider the following thought experiment. During the campaign for the US presidency in 2016, the text of an interview with Donald Trump, candidate for the Republicans, emerged. The interview is dated 1998 and was published the *People* magazine. In it, Trump says:

If I were to run, I'd run as a Republican.
They're the dumbest group of voters in the country.
They believe anything on Fox News.

I could lie and they'd still eat it up.
I bet my numbers would be terrific.

Suppose you are a committed opponent of Donald Trump because Trump goes against all the values you hold dear. The chances are that you see this message as a confirmation of your conviction that Trump is morally wrong. You are sensitive to this particular kind of information because your values are confirmed by it, and because you are relatively quick to accept it as the right information. Furthermore, suppose that you learn that this message is 100% fake, which it is—Trump has never said it. Then, chances are that you will forgive yourself; the message is indeed fake but, you may think, it could have been true.

In her analysis of search behaviour, Galef distinguishes between the mindset of a soldier and that of a scout.[15] Soldiers want to be right and want to win, and mainly look for information that confirms their own views. Scouts continue to search for new information, even though they do not know where it will lead them. After all, a scout wants to know as precisely as possible what a particular area looks like. Most people behave like soldiers, although there are also scouts.

There is an important nuance here. The two navigation systems (analytical/scout and value-based/soldier) are not completely mutually exclusive. Research in news consumption shows that social networks and search engines may contribute to more ideological opposition because users seek to confirm their own opinions. But, because of the variety of available information, they are simultaneously exposed to convictions that are different from their own.[16]

15   Galef, J. (2021). *The Scout Mindset: Why Some People See Things Clearly and Others Don't*, London: Penguin.
16   Flaxman, S., Goel, S., and Rao, J. M. (2016). Filter Bubbles, Echo Chambers and Online News Consumption, Public Opinion Quarterly, *80*(S1), pp. 298–320.

Step two: attention-based business models and their algorithms.
The first observation is a social-psychological mechanism and is not related to technology. I will now conduct a thought experiment, based on information about YouTube strategies for getting more attention.[17] Imagine a platform, which hosts videos, developing a recommendation algorithm with the following, seemingly neutral characteristics:

- The algorithm does not reward the number of clicks to a video but, rather, the viewing time. This is an incentive for makers to produce videos that will be watched for the longest possible time.
- Subsequently, each video-maker is given consent to run ads and these makers also make money through these advertisements in accordance with user viewing times. The financial incentives for the platform and the creators of videos are, as such, fully aligned; everybody has an interest in increased viewing time because everybody makes money accordingly.
- Algorithms are built that identify adjacent relationships between videos. Therefore, users are referred to similar videos, which will lead to a further grip on their attention.
- The risk of this is that viewers get bored. That is why a next-level algorithm is being introduced, that of "reinforcement learning", based on the mechanism of "connecting-to" and "stretching-of". The algorithm predicts which recommendations are in line with users' preferences ("connecting-to"), but may also stretch these preferences ("stretching-of"). As such, the algorithm leads the viewer to different content every time, in order to prevent boredom.

*Step th*ree: *hopping around and wandering in the same world, facilitated by the tree-like structure of ideas.* These are seemingly neutral rules. However, let us continue the thought experiment. Suppose that there is a community of video producers with the

17   Roose, K. (June 8, 2019). *The Making of a YouTube Radical*, The New York Times.

following characteristics: (1) the videos often contain inflammatory messages, (2) they all have a particular underlying philosophy, and (3) this philosophy is applied to a host of themes, including sports, politics, education, culture, history, et cetera. Here, a metaphor of a tree helps; the tree has roots (e.g., a right-extremist or left-extremist ideology) and branches, areas of life where the ideology may be applied.

In such an environment, reinforcement learning may lead to the attention of users being held for a long time. Users may hop from one theme to another (from branch to branch) in order to continuously hear a message that is rooted in the same philosophy, but that is being applied to another domain.

Suppose that a number of these branches contain misleading content. Misleading content often attracts more attention than verified information does. Misleading messages often come with emotion and anger, and this invariably garners more attention than the cold, analytical message that are often inherent to verified information.[18] Algorithms lead users to the branches where the most activity exists—these may be the branches where the most misleading content is being offered. The result is that the user will not only hop from one branch to another, but also to those branches that offer misleading content.

In summary, video providers use attention-based business model. Making videos that are in line with this landscape pays, but with the consequence that users can continue to roam in the imaginary tree-structure. Moreover, this incentive structure is also in line with the social-psychological mechanism whereby users seek information that is appropriate to their own values and preconceptions (the first observation).

Step four: via scent trails to rabbit holes. When I add the first three mechanisms, we see the following:

18 Susarla, A. (January 28, 2020). *Hate cancel culture? Blame algorithms*, The Conversation.

1. users use their values and preconceptions as a navigation system on the Internet—they are soldiers, not scouts, searching for information that is in line with their values;
2. tree-structures of information are available, structures that are rooted in a particular value system—within this system, users may roam for extended periods;
3. significant economic incentives exist for making viewing times as long as possible since viewing time equals adverts and adverts equal income—and, therefore, there are strong incentives to offer attractive videos (producers) and for users to roam within the tree-structure for extended periods;
4. reinforcement learning means that users are continuously offered recommendations in order to pay attention to a particular kind of information, and the tree-structure enables an offer of a variety of information, rooted in the same body of thought.

When sufficient users seek ever-increasing radical content, other users will follow because the algorithms direct them to information that involves a lot of activity. The well-known metaphor that can be used here if of a scent trail of termites.[19] How do termites build a termite mound knowing that there is no central command structure and no leader? It starts with thousands of termites swarming around randomly and continuously leaving scent tracks. When a limited number of them follow the same route, they leave a stronger scent track and others start to follow this same route because of the stronger scent. By following the scent track, they stimulate more and more termites to also follow this route. Each termite carries sand, drops it, and reinforces the scent trail on the spot where the sand is left behind. In this way, other termites know that they must also drop sand at that spot, thus creating a termite mound.

The application of this metaphor to Internet users will be obvious. As more users follow a trail to certain information,

19   de Bruijn, H (2012). *Managing Professionals*, London: Routledge.

others will take the same trail and eventually arrive at the same place. As such, users go through the three I's and might end up with experiencing the "I" of isolation, that is, in a "rabbit hole"—a metaphor derived from the first chapter of *Alice's Adventures in Wonderland* in which Alice follows the White Rabbit to its hole and ends up in an entirely different world. Users who end up in a rabbit hole become prisoners in a surrealistic environment, a parallel universe, in which there is no room for variety and where their own preconceptions are continuously confirmed.

Step five: incentives to stay within the rabbit hole. So, the rabbit hole may occur through a mix of social-psychological, economic, and technical factors whereby cause and effect are often hard to distinguish. There are many more examples of algorithms paving the way to the rabbit hole, but also of algorithms incentivizing users to stay in the rabbit hole as long as possible. How? Again, a service is offered through seemingly neutral rules. Yet a mixture of technological, economic, and social-psychological factors may lead to very dangerous consequences. For example, the creation of private groups:[20]

- Facebook allows the creation of private groups, regardless of whether they are interested in vegan cuisine, kitesurfing, or in endangered species.
- The service is available to everyone, and thus it may also be used by groups spreading misinformation or by groups with extremist ideas who deem violence to be an acceptable strategy.
- Facebook algorithms lead users to these groups,[21] and lead users towards places of high activity. Often, fringe groups with their anger and outrage generate more activity than

20   Roose, K. (July 17, 2017). *Behind the Velvet Ropes of Facebook's Private Groups*, The New York Times.
21   Ovide, S. (August 17, 2020). *Toxic Trade-Offs at Facebook*, The New York Times.

groups that voice mainstream opinions.[22] Also, the mere fact that people participate in a homogeneous group can lead them to take more extreme positions.[23]

- Facebook's own internal research in 2016 found that '64% of all extremist group joins are due to our recommendation tools', primarily through the same "Groups you should join" and "Discover" algorithms. Facebook's algorithms recommended a QAnon group to a *Guardian* reporter's account after the reporter had joined pro-Trump, anti-vaccine, and anti-lockdown Facebook groups.[24]

- These particular groups also organize themselves in the "real world" but, thanks to their online presence, they can make a tremendous jump in scale.

- This process may be bolstered by the algorithm that is directing the newsfeed concerned. When it mainly shows posts of group members—or users' connections—there is the chance that group members are continuously fed similar information.[25]

- A jump in scale may occur by actors who exploit these mechanisms. Consider three examples:
  - Trolling. In 2016, hundreds of Russian trolls pretended to be US citizens on social media. They created Facebook groups around sensitive political themes in the US. Buchanan provides examples of these, including

22 Caveen, S. M. (2021). *Polarflation: The Inflationary Effect of Attention-Optimising Algorithms on Polarisation in the Public Sphere*, London: Media@LSE MSc Dissertation Series.

23 Persily, N., and Tucker, J. A. (2020). *Social Media and Democracy: The State of the Field, Prospects for Reform*, Cambridge: Cambridge University Press.

24 Horwitz, J., and Seetharaman, D. (May 16, 2020). *Facebook executives shut down efforts to make the site less divisive*, The Wall Street Journal.

25 Zollo, F., and Quattrociocchi, W. (2018). Misinformation spreading on Facebook. In S. Lehmann and Y-Y., Ahn (Eds), *Complex Spreading Phenomena in Social Systems*. Springer, pp. 177–196.; Stöcker, C. (2020). How Facebook and Google Accidentally Created a Perfect Ecosystem for Targeted Disinformation. In C. Grimme, M. Preuss, F. W. Takes, and A. Waldherr (Eds.), *Proceedings of MISDOOM 2019: Disinformation in Open Online Media*, Berlin: Springer, pp. 129–149.

Secured Borders, Blacktivist, United Muslims of America, Army of Jesus, and Heart of Texas.[26] Blacktivist alone had generated 11.2 million engagements on Facebook at one time.[27]

- Hostile and weaponized narratives. Radical group members can develop hostile narratives—false stories, that are constructed in such a way that they exploit the fears, anger, or prejudices of users (often the fear of losing wealth, health or identity). Weaponized narratives are focused on incriminating identity and institutions. These stories can subsequently be deployed with users who are sensitive to these particular issues,[28] including users who have ended up in a rabbit hole.

- Slow "red pills". People with radical views can start an Instagram group that offers mainstream conservative news aimed at, for example, conservative followers. By cleverly reposting other people's posts, the initiators try to gather as many followers as possible. The initiators regularly post radical right-wing messages between mainstream news, including messages that concern racism, antisemitism, and conspiracy theories. These do not stay up for long (because followers protest), but they do keep coming back. After a certain period—for example, a year—these radical messages start to dominate, which usually means the end of the group because it is consequently removed by the platform. The initiators of the group then start another group. The idea is that the increasing dosage of radical news, within a context

26   Freedland, J. (August 20, 2020). *Disinformed to death*, The New York Review of Books. https://www.nybooks.com/articles/2020/08/20/fake-news-disinformed-to-death/.
27   H.R.6 – *American Dream and Promise Act* of 2021.
28   Flore, M. (2020). *Understanding Citizens' Vulnerabilities (II): from Disinformation to Hostile Narratives*, Luxembourg: European Commission.

of mainstream news, can make certain followers more sensitive to this radical news.[29]

As such, a technology-driven, neutral service becomes a vehicle for, in this example, the incitement of hate and violence.

These lock-in mechanisms show how fundamentally different the concept of privacy is when compared with the pre-Web world version. Users' personal data leads to their profiling, which can be used to manipulate them (for example through the lock-in mechanisms) and is an example of a type 3 privacy invasion. This does not only have consequences for the individual, but also for the collective (type 4 privacy violations)—lock-in mechanisms can have a far-reaching impact on society. Recommendation systems are 'traps', which are aimed at 'hooking people', and there is also the art of 'captology' (computing products designed to change people's beliefs), the rise of 'captivation metrics', and the emergence of 'cultures of capture'.[30]

Patterns: locking-out

The second pattern is "locking-out". Based on their personal data, users are being excluded from particular services or information. What follows is an overview of types of exclusion.[31]

Withholding information and discrimination. Data can be used to exclude certain users from information and, as such, from particular services. This can happen intentionally but may also be the result of a choice of an algorithm that has been trained with too much historical data—thereby confirming existing discrimination. Well-known examples are:

29   Citarella, J. (July 15, 2021). *There's a new tactic for exposing you to radical content online: the 'slow red-pill'*, The Guardian.
30   Seaver, N. (2019). Captivating algorithms: Recommender systems as traps. *Journal of Material Culture*, 24(4), pp. 421–436.
31   Murphy, L. W., and Cacace, M. (2020). *Facebook's civil rights audit – Final report.* https://about.fb.com/wp-content/uploads/2020/07/Civil-Rights-Audit-Final-Report.pdf

- Housing ads are not offered to users living in a particular zip code.[32] A consequence may be that these ads are not offered to people of colour. When properties are rented mainly by people from minority backgrounds, and the algorithm learns this, the chances are that individuals within these minority groups will not be offered any houses to buy.
- Employment adds are distributed with an algorithm, which mainly directs the ads to male candidates, thus creating gender discrimination. When an existing population of physicians is dominated by males, the algorithm learns that it gets more clicks or views when the advertisement is offered to men.[33]
- The provision of credit may lead to similar mechanisms. An algorithm learns that providing credit to applicants of certain characteristics is high-risk and precludes all applicants with those characteristics.
- Enforcement or predictive policing may be based on data that reflects discriminatory behaviour.[34] The algorithm is trained with data on, for example, control, while this particular control contains a tradition of biased selection of those inspected.
- More generally, groups perceived as unimportant may be denied certain political information, thereby reinforcing existing power gaps.[35] Alternatively, voters do not see that

32 Ali, M., Sapiezynski, P., Bogen, M., Korolova, A., Mislove, A., and Rieke, A. (2019). Discrimination through Optimization: How Facebook's Ad Delivery Can Lead to Biased Outcomes. Proceedings of the ACM on Human-Computer Interaction, 3(CSCW), pp. 1–30.

33 Datta, A., and Tschantz, M. C. (March 17, 2015). *Automated experiments on ad privacy settings: A tale of opacity, choice, and discrimination*, arXiv, https://arxiv.org/abs/1408.6491.

34 Richardson, R., Schultz, J. M., and Crawford, K. (2019). Dirty data, bad predictions: How civil rights violations impact police data, predictive policing systems, and justice. *New York University Law Review, 94*, pp. 192–233.

35 Zarouali, B., Dobber, T., De Pauw, G., and de Vreese, C. (2020). Using a Personality-Profiling Algorithm to Investigate Political Microtargeting: Assessing

their party is conducting a very negative campaign with questionable facts, that is aimed at other voters.[36]

Spreading false information. Data is being used in order to bombard users with disinformation—sometimes this bombardment is quite focused, sometimes less so. In both cases, the disinformation invariably concerns attempts to exclude or deactivate users by discouraging them to assume their rights. Well-known examples are:

– Voter suppression. This may entail the spreading of false information about, for example, polling stations, in order to keep certain voters away from the voting booth. But voter suppression can also be more content based. Data is being used to identify voters who are doubting whether to give a particular candidate their support. The candidate of the opposition may bombard these voters with dubious or malicious information with the objective of refraining from voting. Here too, malicious foreign actors may emerge. Think of Russia's "coordinated deceptive behaviour" in Western countries' elections.

– Census interference is a typical US phenomenon, but it shows how exclusion can occur. The division of seats in the House of Representatives and the division of public resources are based upon de census result. Citizens share data during the census, which cannot be used for law enforcement. Through deploying disinformation in a targeted manner, stating data is indeed used for law enforcement—particular citizens are deterred and refrain from sharing their data.

– Hate speech. Data is being used to inundate certain individuals' or groups' mailboxes with hate-mail and e-mail

the Persuasion Effects of Personality-Tailored Ads on Social Media, *Communication Research*, doi: 0093650220961965.

36 Zarouali, B., Dobber, T., De Pauw, G., and de Vreese, C. (2020). Using a Personality-Profiling Algorithm to Investigate Political Microtargeting: Assessing the Persuasion Effects of Personality-Tailored Ads on Social Media, *Communication Research*, doi: 0093650220961965.

threats. Think of the previously mentioned phenomenon of doxing, whereby a person's data is being used to intimidate the person.

All occurrences above are examples of type 3 and type 4 privacy violations. Individuals hand over data, which may be used for exclusion, and this has both consequences for the individual users' privacy violation (type 3) as well as for society as a whole (type 4).

Moreover, algorithms may also lead to exclusion in a wholly unforeseen manner. A Dutch political party (DENK, literally translated: 'Think') with many voters of Turkish descent, campaigns under the slogan 'Do you want to halt Islam's enemies? Vote DENK!'

The party also advertises in Turkey, to reach Dutch voters of Turkish descent living there. A young Dutch–Turkish author published a novel in the Netherlands, in which she heavily criticized her Islamic upbringing. The book was critically reviewed in a Turkish newspaper. Subsequently, the algorithm placed the political party's advert above the review.[37] The perception that might occur is that someone writes a critical book about her Islamic upbringing and is subsequently branded "an enemy of the Islam", one who needs to be halted. This can be extraordinarily intimidating—also because some people may take the "halting" of the "enemy of Islam" literally.

6.4 Empowerment downstream: how can a user weaponize against locking-in and locking-out?

The essence of the answer to this question is twofold:
(1) awareness, whereby a user is conscious of the process of locking-in and locking-out, and
(2) action, whereby users have options to resist these processes.

37 https://netherlandsnewslive.com/turkish-writer-23-who-is-threatened-with-death-lashes-out-at-denk-om-advertisement-inland/108472/

Empowerment as awareness: locking-in

Empowerment means that users are becoming aware of their value-based selection of information and of the impact of their data-based profiles. Due to these mechanisms, they are more receptive to misleading content. They can be empowered when they know what strategies are being used to spread misleading content or to feed their belief in the value-based selection of information.

- Facts facilitate fake. Misleading information almost always contains a few factual elements, which is given a manipulative twist. Awareness entails users knowing that misleading is often the product of a subtle combination of "fact" and "fake". The function of facts is that they facilitate "fake".

- Laundering information. An actor creates disinformation, and the source of this information is obscured as soon as the information is picked up by others. For instance, a story is constructed on a Russian news site, US citizens on social media pick up on this and the story goes viral. Subsequently, the Russians make sure that the original source of the news can no longer be traced.

- Volume outranks verification. Flooding the information zone is a strategy in which a false narrative is created, which is spread over as many channels as possible, with the aim of overwhelming users. Through an enormous volume of fake news, the impression may occur that it contains a grain of truth. It is important that users realize that volume always requires verification.

- First impressions are powerful. Strategies such as flooding the information zone may lead to a false narrative being the first information to reach a user; 'research suggests that an individual is more likely to recall and internalize the initial information they are exposed to on a divisive topic (...). First impressions are very resilient.'[38] Awareness means that users realize they are sensitive to the power of first impressions.

- The extremes are screaming, while the majority whispers. Often, trolls are active and use misleading information around 'hot button' issues, issues that concern existing and deep contradictions within a society.[39] These contribute, among other things, to increasing the volume of radical messages: 'In our estimate, today the automated accounts at the far left and far right extremes of the US political spectrum produce as many as 25 to 30 times the number of messages per day on average as genuine political accounts across the mainstream.'[40] Again, this is something to be aware of; 'the extremes are screaming while the majority whispers'.[41]

- The use of competing false narratives. In order to veil certain facts, the strategy of competing false narratives is used. In 2014, Malaysia Airlines Flight 17 was shot down over Ukraine. Immediately, a number of entirely different stories were launched on social media. These concerned a plot by the CIA, an explosion on board the plane, and Ukrainian jetfighters being in the vicinity of the aircraft—as such, the image that there is no unilateral, unambiguous explanation for the disaster was subsequently created: 'It's not the purpose to persuade someone with one version of events. The goal for Russia is to achieve a state in which the average media

38 Congress of the United States. (2020). *Report of the Select Committee on Intelligence United States Senate on Russian Active Measures Campaigns and Interference in the 2016 U.S. Election: Volume 2: Russia's Use of Social Media, with Additional Views*, Washington: Congress of the United States (p. 16).

39 Congress of the United States. (2020). *Report of the Select Committee on Intelligence United States Senate on Russian Active Measures Campaigns and Interference in the 2016 U.S. Election: Volume 2: Russia's Use of Social Media, with Additional Views*, Washington: Congress of the United States (p. 6).

40 Congress of the United States. (2018). *Hearing before the Select Committee on Intelligence of the United States Senate One Hundred Fifteenth Congress Second Session*, Washington: Congress of the United States

41 Social media researcher John Kelly—via Congress, op.cit., p. 11.

consumer says, "There are too many versions of events, and I'll never know the truth".[42]

The latter is an important notion, which we also find in the literature about microtargeting. Sometimes the objective is not to influence users in terms of content, but to mobilize or demobilize people—for example, by motivating them to refrain from going to the voting booth.[43] Awareness means that users are conscious of the fact that they are bombarded with tailored information, which is not only directed towards content-driven influencing, but also towards making them demotivated or cynical.

For each of these strategies, it may be so that user data is crucial—the information is then micro-targeted. It is delivered to the users who are, according to their profile, receptive to particular information, allowing the occurrence of the type 3 and 4 privacy violations. But sometimes this is not the case, as "flooding the information zone" may also mean that particular information is simply spread in a massive fashion. There is no precision-shot involved, but with a shot of hail—the sender will eventually see where the misinformation is effective.

For the awareness of the individual user, this does not really make a big difference. Sometimes information is microtargeted, sometimes it is part of a flood, sometimes users will not even know why and how information ends up on their screen. For each of these cases, the impact of type 3 and type 4 privacy violations may diminish when users are aware of these mechanisms.

42 Kalensky, J. (2020). *Report of the Select Committee on Intelligence United States Senate on Russian Active Measures Campaigns and Interference in the 2016 U.S. Election: Volume 2: Russia's Use of Social Media, with Additional Views*, Washington: Congress of the United States. (p. 20).
43 Howard, P. (2020). *Lie Machines: How to Save Democracy from Troll Armies, Deceitful Robots, Junk News Operations, and Political Operatives*, New Haven: Yale University Press.

Empowerment as awareness: locking-out

Where locking-out and awareness are concerned, it helps when users know how their data is being used to lock out certain users, to discriminate against them in a manner that is hardly visible—through the black box of algorithms and data. Awareness means that users are conscious of these biases and black boxes and that they realize that,[44]

- decisions are being made by algorithms, without any human interference to speak of;
- data about users may thus lead to them being profiled and manipulated in the form of locking-out, in which a limited dataset about a user (for instance gender, income, zip code) can sometimes suffice for locking-out;
- here, there may be "dirty data" involved (the familiar example concerns police-officer bias and its influence on police-data meaning, therefore, that algorithmic decision-making is also biased);
- algorithms, apart from the aforementioned dirty data, may also develop biases of their own accord, which is not always easy to trace, not even for experts;
- often, there is no "easy fix" for this problem and that, even when social identifiers (such as gender and colour) are removed from a dataset, there is still sufficient data that remains that contains information about these identifiers.[45]
- The manner in which algorithms take decisions cannot even be comprehended by experts—and that, as such, it

44 Benjamin, R. (2019). *Race After Technology: Abolitionist Tools for the New Jim Code*, Cambridge: Polity Press.; Umoja, N. S. (2018). *Algorithms of Oppression: How Search Engines Reinforce Racism*, New York: University Press.; Thomas, R. (2019). *Getting Specific About Algorithmic Bias*, https://www.youtube.com/watch?v=S-6YGPrmtYc
45 Williams, B. A., Brooks, C. F., and Shmargad, Y. (2018). How Algorithms Discriminate Based on Data They Lack: Challenges, Solutions, and Policy Implications. *Journal of Information Policy, 8*, pp. 78–115.

is hard to retrace whether this decision-making may be biased.

In the above, empowerment mainly means that the user comprehends how processes of locking-in and locking-out run, and which strategies are being applied. The ensuing question is: What action can a user undertake?

Empowerment as action: locking-in

In system theory, there exists the concept of "social-cognitive configurations", whereby a configuration is characterized by a relatively stable pattern of interaction (the social component) and steady, shared perceptions of reality (the cognitive component). In this particular configuration, "fixations" may occur, whereby someone is continuously present in the same social-cognitive configuration, interacts with the same people, and continuously confirms the same perceptions and opinions—the infamous "bubble". That is why "multiple inclusion" is important, meaning that a person should participate in various configurations simultaneously and, as such, is confronted with a variety of actors (the social component) and with a variety of opinions (the cognitive component).[46]

Locking-in is a gradual process in which the users become increasingly connected to a specific social-cognitive configuration. As a member of this configuration, they process information selectively and will accept misleading information more easily. Here, empowerment has two components.

A cognitive component. From a cognitive or cerebral perspective, empowerment involves developing a high tolerance for variety: the ability to process a variety of different data, from an array of

---

46   See, for example, Termeer, C. J. A. M., and Kessener, B. (2007). Revitalizing Stagnated Policy Processes: Using the Configuration Approach for Research and Interventions. *The Journal of Applied Behavioral Science*, *43*(2), pp. 256–272.

perspectives. Empowerment points to the skill of "sense-making", which is defined as 'the ability or attempt to make sense of an ambiguous situation'.[47] Sense-making presupposes the capacity 'to move between heuristics and algorithm, intuition and logic, inductive and deductive reasoning, continuously looking for and providing evidence'.[48]

A social component. Sense-making is, to a great extent, part of a social process—it emerges from an interaction with others.[49] The role of those others is to challenge, test, and modify the person who tries to make sense of a situation.[50] This means that making a connection with others, developing relation networks, and preventing isolation are important to the social component of sense-making.

As said, people simultaneously participating in various configurations are confronted with a variety of actors (the social component) and with a variety of opinions (the cognitive component). Variety is an important safeguard against the danger of lock-in and against biases that can lead to lock-in.[51] Without claiming that it is complete, I present a number of important examples, including the actions they require.
–   Tolerance of conflicting perspectives to prevent oversensitivity to consistency. A line of reasoning can be more or

47   Klein, G., Moon, B., and Hoffman, R. R. (2006). Making Sense of Sensemaking 1: Alternative Perspectives. In IEEE Educational Activities Department, doi: 10.1109/MIS.2006.75.

48   Ancona, D. (2012). Framing and Acting in the Unknown. In S. Snook, N. Nohria, and R. Khurana (Eds.), *The Handbook for Teaching Leadership*, Los Angeles: SAGE Publications.

49   Brown, A.D., Colville, I., and Pye, A. (2015). Making Sense of Sensemaking in Organization Studies. *Organization Studies*, 36(2), pp. 265–277.

50   Ancona, D. (2012). Framing and Acting in the Unknown. In S. Snook, N. Nohria, and R. Khurana (Eds.), *The Handbook for Teaching Leadership*, Los Angeles: SAGE Publications.

51   Heuer, R. J. (1999). *Psychology of Intelligence Analysis*, Central Intelligence Agency: Center for the Study of Intelligence.

less consistent. The bias here that the more consistent a line of reasoning is, the more that it will be perceived as valid. A consistent line of reasoning, with little or selective information, can be of greater impact than a line honouring conflicting perspectives and ambiguous information. The action then becomes to develop a tolerance for conflicting perspectives and information.

– Tolerance of randomness to prevent oversensitivity to causal explanations. The bias then becomes a tendency to identify causal relations, including when they involve random phenomena. A pattern of cause and effect suggests control and creates order in the chaos. From a longing for control and order, the acceptance of randomness can be equated to a lack of understanding. The impact of this bias is that nobody sees causes and effects where there are random phenomena. The action then becomes developing a tolerance for uncertainty and randomness.

– Tolerance of emergence to prevent oversensitivity to a centralized direction. Closely related to the preceding bias, this is the bias to explain events with the aid of explicit decisions of powerful actors such as a central government, the board of a company, or an individual key-player. In reality, decisions are often the result of a series of interactions between a large number of actors. Decisions are not made; they gradually emerge in these multi-actor networks. The action then becomes developing a tolerance for emergence.

– Tolerate the fact that major consequences have minor causes, and vice versa, to prevent oversensitivity to the similarity of cause and effect. The bias here is that small events have limited effects, big events are of high impact, and economic events have economic effects. Again, there is no tolerance whatsoever towards variety—"a big event must have big results". The mighty Spanish Armada was defeated by England—for many Britons, this remains a great historical event, one that has to have been of significant impact. This does not appear to be the case, however, and for many, this is a contra-intuitive fact.[52] The action, in the language of a metaphor is to be tolerant to the fact that the mighty river, raging and tumbling into the sea, began high in the mountains as an unsightly stream.

- Tolerance of external explanations to prevent oversensitivity to internal causes of behaviour. There are internal and external causes of an occurrence. Internal explanations point to the decisions of decision-makers, external explanations relate to the context within which a decision-maker functions. The category of external causes is extremely broad, and a decision-maker only has limited influence on many contextual factors. The bias here is that the role of internal factors is overestimated, and that the role of external factors is underestimated. Closely related to this is the tendency of people to overestimate their own importance. The action here becomes the development of tolerance towards the role of these contextual factors.

- Tolerance of information from different sources to prevent oversensitivity to vivid information. "Vivid" information has, by and large, more impact than abstract information—although this abstract information often is, content-wise, more valuable. In vivid information, concrete, personal information is involved, often in the form of stories, anecdotes, or online videos. Vivid information is also information people receive directly, within a dialogue, and not through third parties. This may mean that information that a person receives in online groups has a relatively big impact. The personal and concrete experience a person shares—an incident or anger about an incident—may be more of a deciding factor in determining the perception than the generic trend in the statistic. The action then becomes developing a tolerance towards the gathering of information from several, competing sources.

52 Heuer, R. J. (1999). *Psychology of Intelligence Analysis*, Central Intelligence Agency: Center for the Study of Intelligence.

Empowerment as action: locking-out

Victims of locking-in—for example, people on the road towards a rabbit hole—may refer to constitutional liberties, in particular their freedom of speech. Those liberties imply that the victim of intimidation has a free choice to be nurtured by certain information or to spread this information. Of course, certain boundaries are in place—think of legal bans on some forms of hate speech—but their fundamental right to freedom of speech remains.

For the victim of locking-out, the legal deck is stacked differently. Democratic countries have comprehensive legislation against discrimination and exclusion. Users who are confronted with locking-out have, as such, a legal title to oppose exclusion. Moreover, the underlying value of equal treatment and the rejection of discrimination is the cornerstone of the rule of law. People confronted with the relatively new phenomenon of algorithmic discrimination may refer to these fundamental rights and values.

Here, empowerment mainly means that users activate their rights. Which actions can be undertaken to this effect?

– Primarily, the mere fact that there is a public debate about the impact of algorithms and that individuals and groups ask attention to processes of exclusion, may already have a positive impact. After all, in the debate, the fundamental anti-discriminatory principle can be referred to, which can activate governments, companies, and social organizations to fight discrimination. In line with this, it can be said that algorithms have 'the allure of objectivity without public accountability',[53] and so it is important that the responsibility of the use of algorithms is properly organized. This too is an important aspect of the public debate.

53   Benjamin, R. (2019). *Race After Technology: Abolitionist Tools for the New Jim Code*, Cambridge: Polity Press (p. 53).

- Demands can be made on algorithmic decision-making. Here, we can identify three directions in general terms:
  - Making algorithmic decision-making more transparent. Benjamin advocates 'coded equity audits' to find biases.[54] There are techniques that can be used to neutralize biases.,[55] There is the concept of Explainable AI (XAI), whereby offering transparency about the function of the algorithm and the data used means that possible bias in the algorithmic decision-making can be ascertained. Although one should not have too high an expectation of XAI (XAI reaches its boundaries fairly quickly, because even experts cannot fathom exactly what an algorithm does), it may, however, contribute to tracing patterns of exclusion. The development of algorithms that can identify hate speech is also in line with this development.[56]
  - Creating more space for non-algorithmic decision-making, either as an alternative to or in addition to algorithmic decision-making.[57] Think of activating the right to a human view—of professionals and/or of target groups. Professionals who make decisions know their professional expertise and intuitions, which may lead to different decisions than those made by algorithms. An important aspect of algorithmic decision-making is the fact that certain groups will be more dependent on it than others. It is plausible

54 Benjamin, R. (2019). *Race After Technology: Abolitionist Tools for the New Jim Code*, Cambridge: Polity Press. (p. 185).

55 Baer, T. (2019). *Understand, Manage, and Prevent Algorithmic Bias*, Berkeley: Apress. (pp. 153–157).

56 Laaksonen, S-M., Haapoja, J., Kinnunen, T., Nelimarkka, M., and Pöyhtäri, R. (2020). The Datafication of Hate: Expectations and Challenges in Automated Hate Speech Monitoring. *Frontiers in Big Data, 3*, pp. 1–3, doi: 10.3389/fdata.2020.00003.

57 Baer, T. (2019). *Understand, Manage, and Prevent Algorithmic Bias*, Berkeley: Apress. (pp. 109–114).

that representatives of these groups participate in the reviewing of algorithms.[58]

- Organizing societal counterforces. Users can mobilize and undertake action against exclusion. The app YikYak enables an exchange of messages within a range of eight kilometres. In practice, this leads to cyber bullying, including racism, for instance, in schools. The app was discontinued following considerable criticism from society. In June 2015, approximately 1,000 Danes formed the Facebook group "Stop Fake Hate Profiles on Facebook". They identified Facebook messages that incite hate against Muslims. People adopted a fictive Islamic identity and subsequently spread messages about killing non-Muslims, raping women, and eventually overtaking Denmark. The members of the Facebook group reported their findings to Facebook and, subsequently and Facebook undertook action against the hate speech.[59]

6.5   Resilience and the role of government

This chapter mainly focused on user empowerment. As such, the chapter is less tool-oriented than the previous chapters. In state- and market-based interventions, instruments can be deployed. Where the empowerment of users, communities, or society as a whole is concerned, the focus mainly lies on creating awareness among users and developing their skills and competencies. Often, this is somewhat less concrete but, as such, no less important.

58   Benjamin, R. (2019). *Race After Technology: Abolitionist Tools for the New Jim Code*, Cambridge: Polity Press. (p. 158).
59   Farkas, J., and C. Neumayer (2017). 'Stop Fake Hate Profiles on Facebook': Challenges for crowdsourced activism on social media. *First Monday*, 22(9), https://doi.org/10.5210/fm.v22i9.8042

This leads to more resilience in protecting privacy, in two senses.

First, data is collected upstream, which can be used midstream and downstream to profile users (type 2 privacy invasion), intimidate them (type 3), and have collective effects (type 4). Empowerment is a typical example of a downstream intervention—users who have been profiled are empowered to recognize and combat manipulation.

Second, empowerment can also lead to redundancy. The more users are empowered, the larger the number of actors who are alert to locking-in and locking-out. Additionally, empowered users are not just less susceptible to the various types of privacy breaches, they are also likely to be more motivated to prevent them—both downstream and upstream. The more users or communities that are empowered, the more redundant the countervailing powers will be to those who collect data and invade privacy.

Governments can use various policy instruments:
- legal instrument, obligations to make privacy conditions explicit, or of regulations that forbid discrimination that be deployed in the fight against locking-out mechanisms;
- economic instruments, financial support for consumer organizations and educational programmes or financial penalties for violations that may lead to privacy violations
- communicative instruments, constantly emphasizing the importance of privacy (think of the yearning for the sea), developing information, and education campaigns, investing in 21st-century digital skills.

Again, this instruments may be less concrete than the instruments mentioned the previous chapters, but they are no less important.

7   Reflections

II will conclude this discourse on the governance of privacy with two brief reflections.

The first reflection concerns the tension between the global reach of the tech giants and the limited reach of national governments' interventions, while the second reflection concerns the normative dimension of the governance of privacy.

Global players versus national governments

The first reflection concerns the tension between the global reach of the tech giants and the limited jurisdiction of national governments. This imbalance often favours tech giants, who can use their power to put pressure on national governments. One example of this it the clash between Facebook and the Australian government in 2021. Facebook blocked news to Australian users in response to an Australian law proposal, that would require tech companies to pay for news content.[1] The ban shows the power of the tech giants; such companies are global players, and sometimes openly seek confrontation with national governments.

How can governments deal with this? Of course, it is important that they collaborate in the fight for more privacy protection. Furthermore, the three economic blocks (EU, US, China) are each an important countervailing power against the tech giants. In this reflection, I would like to emphasize the importance of redundancy as a principle of governance. Privacy is a wicked, multi-faceted phenomenon, one that requires a redundant system of interventions for its protection.

1   Bland, A. (24, February 2021). Facebook over-enforced Australia news ban, admits Nick Clegg. *The Guardian* https://www.theguardian.com/technology/2021/feb/24/facebook-over-enforced-australia-news-ban-admits-nick-clegg

Redundancy relates first and foremost to the instruments that governments can deploy. The message of this book is that governments can use the power of the state, the power of the market, and the power of society, and that there is, therefore, a huge variety of instruments at their disposal. . The more instruments there are available, the more possibilities there will be to fight the many-headed monster of privacy invasions. Redundancy means that the limitations of one instrument can be compensated by another. For example, some instruments are bound by national jurisdictions, but others are not (think of the many tools described in Chapter 5). Moreover, a variety of instruments makes it possible to learn: which instruments and which mixes of instruments are effective—and which are not?

Redundancy refers, secondly, to the actors involved in governance. Again, the more actors that are activated to prevent privacy invasions, the more opportunities there will be for privacy protection. Tech giants are global players, while many of the instruments available to governments, are national instruments. This has long been to the advantage of the tech giants because individual national governments often find it difficult to influence such global players. But privacy is now high on the agenda in many countries. For the tech giants, this means being faced with a multitude of interventions by a multitude of national governments aimed at protecting citizens' privacy. A few decades ago, tech giants lived in an under-regulated world, now their world is less comfortable. A tech giant can be a spider in its global web—but if privacy is high on the agenda everywhere, the tech giant has also become a bit of a fly in the global web. Moreover, governments can learn from each other and copy others' best practices. A court decision in a particular country, with a major impact on tech giants, can attract worldwide attention and other countries might then copy this decision.

A redundant system of interventions therefore has a number of advantages. It comprises incentives to protect privacy. If some of these incentives do not work, there are always others that will. Redundancy is a breeding ground for learning processes and an invitation to constantly design new interventions. But there is more: redundancy can also be an answer to the global dominance of the tech giants. By constantly designing new interventions for privacy protection across the globe, tech giants will be increasingly forced to protect the privacy of their users. There is, of course, no guarantee that this will be the case—but redundancy can at least contribute to greater privacy protection.

The dynamics of norms

Second, the effectiveness of privacy governance depends heavily on the legitimacy of the fight for privacy—the recognition that the value of privacy is important and worth striving for. As a reminder (see Chapter 3), privacy protection instruments are embedded in norms, which, in turn, are embedded in values.

An initial observation must be that there is a strong dynamic surrounding the value of privacy.

- Privacy always stands in relation to other values. Sometimes these other values do not detract from the importance of privacy; sometimes a trade-off must be made between privacy and these other values. Sometimes this will be a false choice and other values need not come at the expense of privacy. However, sometimes this is unavoidable.
- This trade-off is influenced by societal beliefs, which are also subject to change. Immediately after a terrorist attack, many citizens are more willing to trade their privacy for more safety and security when compared with peaceful times.
- The trade-off is influenced by technological dynamics. New technologies or new data-based services can require new trade-offs between privacy and other values—sometimes in favour of privacy, sometimes in favour of other values.
- The trade-off is also influenced by the effectiveness of governance. If governance produces many negative and unintended effects, the legitimacy of privacy protection

(Chapter 3) may suffer, and support for the underlying norms may be undermined.

Privacy governance is built on the foundation of a societal consensus about the underlying norms and values. The dynamics described here show that this foundation can be rather shaky. How can this be dealt with? There is no simple answer to this question so, to conclude this book, I offer two considerations using three analogies: drugs policy, environmental policy, and education.

The risk of political polarization

There is a distinction between, roughly speaking, conservative and liberal drug policies. Is drug use a major problem one that should be limited as much as possible, in line with the conservative lens? Or is it the case that not all drug use is wrong and that drug use is, in fact, an individual choice, in line with the liberal lens? The liberal lens implies that an uncompromising fight against the production and sale of drugs is neither effective nor legitimate.

It is conceivable that two such lenses will also develop around data and data use.

Lens 1: data use is a major problem and requires the maximum efforts of governments to limit data use.

Lens 2: data use is not always wrong; it is an individual decision and the fight against data misuse expends too many government resources.

If these two lenses develop, and if they can be linked to political ideologies, this may have serious consequences for the legitimacy of privacy protection. Privacy threatens to become a highly politicized subject with a problematic legitimacy, which, ultimately, might also affect the effectiveness of privacy protection.

What, then, is the way out here? How do you transcend a battle between two schools of thought and prevent politicization and polarization? The answer for drug policy is as follows: by being somewhat cautious and not conducting an uncompromising "war on drugs" but, rather, by making strategic choices concerning priorities. We know this phenomenon from the literature on enforcement. The strategic selection of priorities, the alertness to unintended negative effects (see Chapter 3), the smart use of the limited resources of regulators, all are conducive to the effectiveness and legitimacy of enforcement—the challenge will be no different in the case of privacy protection.

Negative externalities: privacy as a merit good

An individual who is profiled (type 2 privacy invasion) or manipulated (type 3 privacy invasion) may not perceive this as a violation of their privacy. People may, for example, perceive profiling as the inevitable consequence of using certain services. Alternatively, users who have ended up in a rabbit hole mostly have no objection to receiving information that manipulates them further.

However, privacy violations do not only affect individuals, they also effect society as a whole (see Chapters 1 and 6): involving issues such as discrimination, hate speech, rabbit holes, and spreading extremist views. These effects bring to mind a concept from environmental economics: "negative externalities"—the phenomenon that individuals negatively impact society as a whole, without paying the price for doing so. Companies emit toxic substances and make a profit regardless, passing on the environmental damage to society. When negative externalities exist, it is perfectly legitimate for a government to intervene and neutralize these externalities.

If it is true that privacy is not always in good hands with the individual, the "merit good" emerges as an interesting concept. Merit goods are products or services that are deemed by the governments to pose a risk of underconsumption, while consumption of these products provides important positive societal effects; the most familiar example of a merit good is education. Education is hugely significant for the development and future opportunities of individuals, and for society as a whole. Similarly, privacy protection is of great importance for the development of individuals (less profiling, less manipulation) and for society as a whole (fewer negative externalities).

Privacy as merit good means that governments will want the protection of privacy to prevail, even when privacy is of scant concern to individual citizens. If we consider privacy as a merit good then this will, again, show the radical transformation of the concept of privacy. According to the traditional, pre-Web concept of privacy, the individual citizen is in charge. Should privacy develop into a merit good, the governments will imposes the value of privacy on citizens.

References

Acquisti, A., and Grossklags, J. (2005). Privacy and Rationality in Individual Decision Making. *IEEE Security & Privacy*, *3*(1), pp. 26–33.

Acquisti, A., Curtis T., and Wagman, L. (2016). The Economics of Privacy. *Journal of Economic Literature*, *54*(2), pp. 442–492.

Alanoca, S., Guetta-Jeanrenaud, N., Ferrari, I., Weinberg, N., Çetin, R. B., and Miailhe, N. (2021). Digital contact tracing against COVID-19: a governance framework to build trust. *International Data Privacy Law*, *11*(1), pp. 3–17.

Alford, J., and Head, B. W. (2017). Wicked and less wicked problems: a typology and a contingency framework. *Policy and Society*, *36*(3), pp. 397–413, doi: 10.1080/14494035.2017.1361634.

Alger, S. (December 26, 2020). *The Freakout Over Pornhub's Mass Deletion*. The Pink. https://medium.com/the-pink/the-freakout-over-pornhubs-mass-deletion-c9feacb69d6

Ali, M., Sapiezynski, P., Bogen, M., Korolova, A., Mislove, A., and Rieke, A. (2019). Discrimination through Optimization: How Facebook's Ad Delivery Can Lead to Biased Outcomes. Proceedings of the ACM on Human-Computer Interaction, *3*(CSCW), pp. 1–30.

Alonzo, I. (January 14, 2021). *Amazon Prime 'Dark Pattern' of Service Cancellation Explained: Why Consumer Groups Think It's Unfair and Deceptive*, Tech Times. https://www.techtimes.com/articles/255977/20210114/amazon-prime-dark-pattern-service-cancellation-explained-why-consumer-groups.htm

Alpers, S., Betz, S., Fritsch, A., Oberweis, A., Schiefer, G., and Wagner, M. (2018). Citizen Empowerment by a Technical Approach for Privacy Enforcement. In, *Proceedings of the 8th International Conference on Cloud Computing and Services Science* (Vol. 1), CLOSER, pp. 589–595.

Ancona, D. (2012). Framing and Acting in the Unknown. In S. Snook, N. Nohria, and R. Khurana (Eds.), *The Handbook for Teaching Leadership*, Los Angeles: SAGE Publications.

Anderson, R. (September 15, 2020). The Panopticon is Already Here. *The Atlantic*. https://www.theatlantic.com/magazine/archive/2020/09/china-ai-surveillance/614197/

Ash, J. S., Berg, M., and Coiera E. (2004). Some unintended consequences of information technology in health care: the nature of patient care information system-related errors. *Journal of the American Medical Informatics Association*, *11*(2), pp. 104–112.

Ashford, N. A., and Caldart, C. C. (2005). *Negotiated Regulation, Implementation and Compliance in the United States*, New York: Springer.

Baer, T. (2019). *Understand, Manage, and Prevent Algorithmic Bias*, Berkeley: Apress.

Baldwin, R., and Cave, M. (1990). *Understanding Regulation: Theory, Strategy and Practice*, Oxford: Oxford University Press, pp. 101–102.

Barrett, L. (2017). Herbie Fully Downloaded: Data-Driven Vehicles and the Automobile Exception. *Georgetown Law Journal, 106*, pp. 181–208.

Barth, S., and De Jong, M. D. (2017). The privacy paradox: Investigating discrepancies between expressed privacy concerns and actual online behavior—A systematic literature review. *Telematics and informatics, 34*(7), pp. 1038–1058.

Bax, E. (2019). *Computing A Data Dividend.* ACM Economics & Computation 2019, https://arxiv.org/pdf/1905.01805.pdf

Bayer, J. (2020). Double harm to voters: data-driven micro-targeting and democratic public discourse. *Internet Policy Review, 9*(1), pp. 1–17, doi: 10.14763/2020.1.1460.

Becker, M. (2019). Privacy in the digital age: comparing and contrasting individual versus social approaches towards privacy. *Ethics and Information Technology, 21*, pp. 307–317.

Benjamin, R. (2019). *Race After Technology: Abolitionist Tools for the New Jim Code*, Cambridge: Polity Press.

Bertoncello, M., Camplone, G., Mohr, D., Möller, T., Wee, D., Gao, P., and Kaas, H-W. (2016). *Monetizing car data: New service business opportunities to create new customer benefits*, McKinsey & Company.

Bi, B., Shokouhi, M., Kosinski, M., and Graepel, T. (2013). Inferring the demographics of search users: Social data meets search queries. In *Proceedings of the 22nd international conference on World Wide Web*, pp. 131–140.

Bibby, C., Gordon, J., Schuler, G., and Stein, E. (2021). The big reset: Data-driven marketing in the next normal. Munich: McKinsey & Company.

Bisogni, F. (2020). *Information Availability and Data Breaches. Data Breach Notification Laws and Their Effects*, Delft: Delft University of Technology.

Blake, T., Nosko, C., and Tadelis, S. (2015). Consumer Heterogeneity and Paid Search Effectiveness: A Large-Scale Field Experiment. *Econometrica, 83*(1), pp. 155–174.

Bland, A. (24 February 2021). Facebook over-enforced Australia news ban, admits Nick Clegg, *The Guardian* https://www.theguardian.com/technology/2021/feb/24/facebook-over-enforced-australia-news-ban-admits-nick-clegg

Blumenstock, J., Cadamuro, G., and On, R. (2015). Predicting poverty and wealth from mobile phone metadata. *Science, 350*(6264), pp.1073–1076.

Bolton, T., Dargahi, T., Belguith, S., Al-Rakham, M. S., and Sodhro, A. H. (2021). On the Security and Privacy Challenges of Virtual Assistants. *Sensors, 21*(7), p. 2312, doi: 10.3390/s21072312.

Borgogno, O., and Colangelo, G. (2019). Data sharing and interoperability: Fostering innovation and competition through APIs. *Computer Law & Security Review, 35*(5), p. 105314. https://doi.org/10.1016/j.clsr.2019.03.008.

Brown, A.D., Colville, I., and Pye, A. (2015). Making Sense of Sensemaking in Organization Studies. *Organization Studies, 36*(2), pp. 265–277.

Bax, E. (2019). Computing A Data Dividend. *ACM Economics & Computation 2019*, https://arxiv.org/pdf/1905.01805.pdf

de Bruijn, H., and Hufen, H. (1998). The traditional approach to policy instruments. In B. G. Peters, and F. K. M. Nispen (Eds.), *Public Policy Instruments. Evaluating the Tools of Public Administration*, Cheltenham: Edward Elgar.

De Bruijn, H., ten Heuvelhof, E. (1998). A contextual approach to policy instruments. In B. G. Peters, and F. K. M. van Nispen (Eds.), *Public Policy Instruments. Evaluating the Tools of Public Administration*, Cheltenham: Edward Elgar, pp. 69–84.

de Bruijn, H. (2006). *Managing Performance in the Public Sector*, London: Routledge.

de Bruijn, H., ten Heuvelhof, E., and in't Veld, R. (2010). *Process Management*, Berlin: Springer.

de Bruijn, H (2012). *Managing Professionals*, London: Routledge.

de Bruijne, M. L. C., Boin, A., and van Eeten, M. J. G. (2012). Resilience. Exploring the concept and its meaning. In L. K. Comfort, A. Boin, and C. C. Demchak (Eds.), *Designing Resilience. Preparing for Extreme Events*), Pittsburgh: University of Pittsburgh Press, pp. 13–32

Büchi, M., Just, N., and Latzer, M. (2017). Caring is not enough: the importance of Internet skills for online privacy protection. *Information, Communication & Society*, 20(8), pp. 1261–1278.

Bygrave, L.A. (2017). Data protection by Design and by Default: Deciphering the EU's Legislative Requirements. *Oslo Law Review*, 4(2), pp. 105–120.

Cadwalladr, C. (May 7, 2017). The great British Brexit robbery: how our democracy was hijacked, *The Guardian*. https://www.theguardian.com/technology/2017/may/07/the-great-british-brexit-robbery-hijacked-democracy

Cave, M. (2006). Six Degrees of Separation Operation: Separation as a Remedy in European Telecommunications Regulation, *Communications and Strategies*, no. 64, 4th Quarter, pp. 1–15.

Caveen, S. M. (2021). *Polarflation: The Inflationary Effect of Attention-Optimising Algorithms on Polarisation in the Public Sphere*, London: Media@LSE MSc Dissertation Series.

Chen, B. X. (May 23, 2018). *Getting a Flood of GDPR-Related Privacy Policy Updates? Read Them*, The New York Times. https://www.nytimes.com/2018/05/23/technology/personaltech/what-you-should-look-for-europe-data-law.html

Chen, H. T. (2018). Revisiting the privacy paradox on social media with an extended privacy calculus model: The effect of privacy concerns, privacy self-efficacy, and social capital on privacy management. *American Behavioral Scientist*, 62(10), pp.1392–1412.

Chen, Y., Mao, Z., and Qiu, J. L. (2018). *Super-sticky WeChat and Chinese Society*, Bingley: Emerald Publishing.

Cimpanu, C. (October 17, 2019). *Germany's cyber-security agency recommends Firefox as most secure browser*, ZDNet. https://www.zdnet.com/article/germanys-cyber-security-agency-recommends-firefox-as-most-secure-browser/

Citarella, J. (July 15, 2021). *There's a new tactic for exposing you to radical content online: the 'slow red-pill'*, The Guardian. https://www.theguardian.com/commentisfree/2021/jul/15/theres-a-new-tactic-for-exposing-you-to-radical-content-online-the-slow-red-pill

Coglianese, C., Nash, J., and Olmstead, T. (2003). Performance-based regulation: Prospects and limitations in health, safety, and environmental protection, *Administrative Law Review*, 55(4), pp. 705–729.

Coglianese, C. (1997). Assessing consensus: The promise and the Performance of Negotiated Rulemaking. *Duke Law Journal, 46*, pp. 1255–1349.

Cohen, N. (July 2, 2019), *Will California's New Bot Law Strengthen Democracy?*, The New Yorker, The New Yorker. https://www.newyorker.com/tech/annals-of-technology/will-californias-new-bot-law-strengthen-democracy

Congress of the United States. (2018). *Hearing before the Select Committee on Intelligence of the United States Senate One Hundred Fifteenth Congress Second Session*, Washington: Congress of the United States

Congress of the United States. (2020). *Report of the Select Committee on Intelligence United States Senate on Russian Active Measures Campaigns and Interference in the 2016 U.S. Election (Vol 2): Russia's Use of Social Media, with Additional Views*, Washington: Congress of the United States.

Court of Justice of the European Union (16 July 2020), Judgment of the Court, Case C-311/18.

Datta, A., and Tschantz, M. C. (March 17, 2015). *Automated experiments on ad privacy settings: A tale of opacity, choice, and discrimination*, arXiv, https://arxiv.org/abs/1408.6491.

Degli Esposti, S., Ball, K., and Dibb, S. (2021). What's In It For Us? *Benevolence, National Security, and Digital Surveillance, Public Administrative Review, 81*(5), pp. 862–873, doi: 10.1111/puar.13362.

Deighton-Smith, R. (2008). Process and performance-based regulation: challenges for regulatory governance and regulatory reform. In P. Carroll, R. Deighton-Smith, H. Silver, and C. Walker (Eds.), *Minding the Gap*, Canberra: University Printing Services.

Digital Competition Expert Panel. (2019). *Unlocking digital competition*, London: HM Treasury.

Dobber, T., Fathaigh, R. Ó., and Zuiderveen Borgesius, F. (2019). The regulation of online political micro-targeting in Europe, *Internet Policy Review, 8*(4). https://policyreview.info/articles/analysis/regulation-online-political-micro-targeting-europe

van der Doelen, F. C. J. (1998). The "Give-and-Take" Packaging of Policy Instruments: Optimizing Legitimacy and Effectiveness. In M-L. Bemelmans-Videc, R. C. Rist, and E. Vedung (Eds.), *Carrots, Sticks & Sermons*, New York: Routledge.

Doss, A. F. (2020). Cyber Privacy. *Who Has Your Data and Why Should You Care*, Dallas: BenBella Books.

Eaton, J., (2019). *Catholics in Iowa went to church. Steve Bannon tracked their phones*, ThinkProgress, https://archive.thinkprogress.org/exclusive-steve-bannon-geofencing-data-collection-catholic-church-4aaeacd5c182/.

Edelson, L., Lauinger, T., and McCoy, D. (2020). A Security Analysis of the Facebook Ad Library, *2020 IEEE Symposium on Security and Privacy*, pp. 661–678, doi: 10.1109/SP40000.2020.00084.

Editorial Bord New York Times. (February 2, 2019). How Silicon Valley Puts the 'Con' in Consent, The New York Times. https://www.nytimes.com/2019/02/02/opinion/internet-facebook-google-consent.html

Epp, C., Lippold, M., and Mandryk, R. L. (2011). Identifying emotional states using keystroke dynamics, *Proceedings of the SIGCHI Conference on Human Factors in Computing Systems*, pp. 715–724. https://dl.acm.org/doi/10.1145/1978942.1979046

Eubanks, V. (2018). *Automating Inequality*, New York: St. Martin's Press.

European Commission (2018). *Proposal for a Council Directive laying down rules relating to the corporate taxation*, of significant digital presence, Brussels European Commission

Farkas, J., and C. Neumayer (2017). 'Stop Fake Hate Profiles on Facebook': Challenges for crowdsourced activism on social media. *First Monday*, 22(9), https://doi.org/10.5210/fm.v22i9.8042

Flaxman, S., Goel, S., and Rao, J. M. (2016). Filter Bubbles, Echo Chambers and Online News Consumption, Public Opinion Quarterly, *80*(S1), pp. 298–320.

Michèle, F., and Pallas, F. (2020). They who must not be identified—distinguishing personal from non-personal data under the GDPR. *International Data Privacy Law*, *10*(1), pp. 11–36.

Flore, M. (2020). *Understanding Citizens' Vulnerabilities (II): from Disinformation to Hostile Narratives*, Luxembourg: European Commission.

Forbrukerrådet. (2018). *Deceived by design, How tech companies use dark patterns to discourage us from exercising our rights to privacy*, Oslo: Forbrukerrådet.

Foroohar, R. (2019). *Don't Be Evil: The Case Against Big Tech*, Australia: Currency Press.

Freedland, J. (August 20, 2020). *Disinformed to death*, The New York Review of Books. https://www.nybooks.com/articles/2020/08/20/fake-news-disinformed-to-death/

Furey, E., and Blue, J. (2019). *Can I Trust Her? Intelligent Personal Assistants and GDPR, International Symposium on Networks, Computers and Communications* (ISNCC), pp. 1–6. https://ieeexplore.ieee.org/abstract/document/8909098

Galef, J. (2021). *The Scout Mindset: Why Some People See Things Clearly and Others Don't*, London: Penguin.

Gianclaudio, M., and Custers, B. (2018). Pricing privacy – the right to know the value of your personal data, Computer law and Security Review, *34*(2), pp. 289–303.

Goldfarb, A., and Tucker, C. (2012). Privacy and innovation. *Innovation Policy and the Economy*, 12(1), pp. 65–90, doi: 10.1086/663156.

Green, M. D., and Stamos, A. (August 11, 2021). *Guest Essay: Apple Wants to Protect Children. But It's Creating Serious Privacy Risks*, New York Times. https://www.nytimes.com/2021/08/11/opinion/apple-iphones-privacy.html

Gürses, S., and van Hoboken, J. (2017). In J. Polonetsky et al. (Eds.) *Privacy after the agile turn, Cambridge Handbook of Consumer Privacy*. Cambridge: Cambridge University Press.

Harter, P. J. (1982). Negotiating regulations: A cure for malaise, *Georgetown Law Journal*, *71*(1), pp. 75–91, doi:10.1016/S0195-9255(82)80028-0.

Hawkins, K. (1984). *Environment and Enforcement. Regulation and the Social Definition of Pollution*, Oxford: Clarendon Press, pp. 111–113.

Helberger, N., Pierson, J., and Poell, T. (2018). Governing online platforms: From contested to cooperative responsibility, *The Information Society*, *34*(1), pp. 1–14, doi: 10.1080/01972243.2017.1391913.

Hern, A. (November 17, 2019). *Firefox's fight for the future of the web*, The Guardian. https://www.theguardian.com/technology/2019/nov/17/firefox-mozilla-fights-back-against-google-chrome-dominance-privacy-fears

Heuer, R. J. (1999). *Psychology of Intelligence Analysis*, Central Intelligence Agency: Center for the Study of Intelligence.

Hill, K. (November 5, 2019). *I Got Access to My Secret Consumer Score. Now You Can Get Yours, Too*, The New York Times.https://www.nytimes.com/2019/11/04/business/secret-consumer-score-access.html

Hill, K. (2020). *She Will Rise. Becoming a Warrior in the Battle for True Equality*, New York: Grand Central Publishing.

Hitlin, P., and Raine, R. (January 16, 2018). *Facebook Algorithms and Personal Data*, Pew Research Center Internet & Technology.https://www.pewresearch.org/internet/2019/01/16/facebook-algorithms-and-personal-data/

Hodgson, G. M. (2006). What are Institutions? *Journal of Economic Issues, 40*(1), pp. 1–25.

Holderness, H. (2013). Taxing Privacy. *Georgetown Journal on Poverty Law & Policy, 21*(1), pp. 1–41.

Hollnagel, E. (1999). Accident Analysis and Barrier Functions, IFE, pp. 1–34. https://www.it.uu.se/research/project/train/papers/AccidentAnalysis.pdf

Horwitz, J., and Seetharaman, D. (May 16, 2020). *Facebook executives shut down efforts to make the site less divisive*, The Wall Street Journal.https://www.wsj.com/articles/facebook-knows-it-encourages-division-top-executives-nixed-solutions-11590507499

House of Commons. (May 15, 2020). *Briefing Paper Patient health records: access, sharing and confidentiality.* https://commonslibrary.parliament.uk/research-briefings/sn07103/.

Howard, P. (2020). *Lie Machines: How to Save Democracy from Troll Armies, Deceitful Robots, Junk News Operations, and Political Operatives*, New Haven: Yale University Press.

Howlett, M. (2010). *Designing public policies: Principles and instruments*, Abingdon: Routledge.

Hughes, C. (April 27, 2018). *The wealth of our collective data should belong to all of us*, The Guardian.https://www.theguardian.com/commentisfree/2018/apr/27/chris-hughes-facebook-google-data-tax-regulation

Isaac, M. (January 13, 2019). *Apple Shows Facebook Who Has the Power in an App Dispute*, The New York Times.https://www.nytimes.com/2019/01/31/technology/apple-blocks-facebook.html

John, L. K. (September 18, 2018). *Uninformed consent*, Harvard Business Review. https://hbr.org/2018/09/uninformed-consent

Johnson, B. (1996). *Polarity Management*, Amhurst: HRD Press.

Kaesling, K. (2018). Privatising Law Enforcement in Social Networks: A Comparative Model Analysis. *Erasmus Law Review, 3*, pp. 151–164.

Kagan, R. A., and Scholtz, J. T. (1984). The Criminology of the Corporation and regulatory Enforcement Strategies. In K. Hawkins and J. M. Thomas (Eds.), *Enforcing Regulation*, Boston: Kluwer-Nijhoff Publishing.

Kalensky, J. (2020). *Report of the Select Committee on Intelligence United States Senate on Russian Active Measures Campaigns and Interference in the 2016 U.S. Election (Vol.2): Russia's Use of Social Media, with Additional Views*, Washington: Congress of the United States.

Keller, P. (2019). The reconstruction of privacy through law: a strategy of diminishing expectations. *International Data Privacy Law, 9*(3), pp. 132–152.

Kelly, M. (June 26, 2020). *Unilever will pull ads from Facebook, Instagram, and Twitter for the rest of the year*, The Verge.https://www.theverge.com/2020/6/26/21304619/unilever-facebook-instagram-twitter-ad-boycott-spending-dove-hellmans

Khan, L. M. (2017). Amazon's Anti-Trust Paradox. *The Yale Law Journal, 126*(3), pp. 717–722.

Klein, G., Moon, B., and Hoffman, R. R. (2006). Making Sense of Sensemaking 1: Alternative Perspectives. In IEEE Educational Activities Department, Vol. 21. No 4

Kokott, J., and Sobotta, C. (2013). The distinction between privacy and data protection in the jurisprudence of the CJEU and the ECtHR. *International Data Privacy Law, 3*(4), pp. 222–228.

Kosinski, M., Stillwell, D., and Graepel, T. (2013). Private traits and attributes are predictable from digital records of human behavior. *Proceedings of the National Academy of Sciences, 110*(15), pp. 5802–5805.

Kristof, N. (December 4, 2020). *The Children of Pornhub*, The New York Times. https://www.nytimes.com/2020/12/04/opinion/sunday/pornhub-rape-trafficking.html

Krotzek, L. J. (2019). Inside the voter's mind: the effect of psychometric microtargeting on feelings toward and propensity to vote for a candidate. *International Journal of Communication, 13*(21), pp. 3609–3629.

Laaksonen, S-M., Haapoja, J., Kinnunen, T., Nelimarkka, M., and Pöyhtäri, R. (2020). The Datafication of Hate: Expectations and Challenges in Automated Hate Speech Monitoring. *Frontiers in Big Data, 3*, pp. 1–3, doi: 10.3389/fdata.2020.00003.

Lavigne, M. (2020). *Strengthening ties: The influence of microtargeting on partisan attitudes and the vote*, Party Politics, doi: 10.1177/1354068820918387.

Lindsay, R. (October 27, 2020). To Fix Section 230, Target Algorithmic Amplification, The Information.https://www.theinformation.com/articles/to-fix-section-230-target-algorithmic-amplification

Lohr, S. (October 22, 2020). *Forget Antitrust Laws. To Limit Tech, Some Say a New Regulator Is Needed*, The New York Times.https://www.nytimes.com/2020/10/22/technology/antitrust-laws-tech-new-regulator.html

Lynn Jr., L. E., Heinrich, C. J., and Hill, C. J. (2001). Improving Governance: A New Logic for Empirical Research, Washington DC: Georgetown University Press.

Marian, O. Y. (2021). Taxing Data. *UC Irvine School of Law Research Paper Series, 17*, pp. 53–54.

Morozov, E. (May 15, 2021). *Privacy activists are winning fights with tech giants. Why does victory feel hollow?*, The Guardian.https://www.theguardian.com/commentisfree/2021/may/15/privacy-activists-fight-big-tech

Mukherjee, A. (May 23, 2020). *China's Crypto Is All About Tracing — and Power*, BloombergOpinion.https://www.bnnbloomberg.ca/china-s-crypto-is-all-about-tracing-and-power-1.1440331

Murphy, L. W., and Cacace, M. (2020). *Facebook's civil rights audit – Final report*. https://about.fb.com/wp-content/uploads/2020/07/Civil-Rights-Audit-Final-Report.pdf.

Narayanan, A., and Shmatikov, V. (2008). *Robust de-anonymization of large sparse datasets*, 2008 IEEE Symposium on Security and Privacy, pp. 111–125.https://ieeexplore.ieee.org/document/4531148

Neumann, N., Tucker, C. E., and Whitfield, T. (2019). How Effective is Third-party consumer profiling and audience delivery?: Evidence from field studies. *Marketing Science-Frontiers*, Vol 38(6): pp. 918-926

Nissenbaum, H. (2010). *Privacy in Context: Technology, Policy and the Integrity of Social Life*, Palo Alto: Stanford University Press.

Nissenbaum, H. (2015). Respect for context as a benchmark for privacy online: What it is and isn't? In B. Roessler and D. Mokrosinska (Eds.), *Social Dimensions of Privacy: Interdisciplinary Perspectives* (pp. 278–302). Cambridge: Cambridge University Press.

North, D. C. (1990). *Institutions, Institutional Change and Economic Performance*. Cambridge. Cambridge University Press.

Oremus, W. (2019). *How Much Is Your Privacy Really Worth?* OneZero. https://onezero.medium.com/how-much-is-your-privacy-really-worth-421796dd9220.

Ovide, S. (August 17, 2020). *Toxic Trade-Offs at Facebook*, The New York Times. https://www.nytimes.com/2020/08/17/technology/facebook-qanon.html

Persily, N., and Tucker, J. A. (2020). *Social Media and Democracy: The State of the Field, Prospects for Reform*, Cambridge: Cambridge University Press.

Pierson J. (2015) Privacy and Empowerment in Connective Media. In: Tiropanis T., Vakali A., Sartori L., Burnap P. (eds) Internet Science. INSCI 2015. *Lecture Notes in Computer Science,* vol 9089. Springer, Cham. https://doi.org/10.1007/978-3-319-18609-2_1

Plunkett, A. L. (2019). *Sharenthood: Why We Should Think before We Talk About Our Kids Online*, Boston: MIT Press.

Priest, D. (n. d.). *Google and Facebook treating your data like property would be terrible – CNET*. https://www.cnet.com/news/google-and-facebook-treating-your-data-like-property-would-be-terrible/

Privacy International (n. d.). *Examples of Data Points Used in Profiling*, https://privacyinternational.org/sites/default/files/2018-04/data%20points%20used%20in%20tracking_0.pdf

Powell, W. (1990). Neither market nor hierarchy: Network forms of organization. In L. L. Cummings, and B. M. Staw (Eds.), *Research in Organizational Behavior*, Greenwich: JAI Press, pp. 295–366.

Rerup, C. (2001). "Houston, we have a problem": Anticipation and improvisation as sources of organizational resilience', *Comportamiento Organizacional e Gestao, 7*(1), pp. 27–44.

Richardson, R., Schultz, J. M., and Crawford, K. (2019). Dirty data, bad predictions: How civil rights violations impact police data, predictive policing systems, and justice. *New York University Law Review, 94*, pp. 192–233.

Roderick, R. (February 22, 2019). *YouTube's Latest Child Controversy Has Kick-Started A War Over How To Fix The Platform*, BuzzFeed.News. https://www.buzzfeednews.com/article/ryanhatesthis/youtube-child-sexual-exploitation-creators-watson

Roose, K. (July 17, 2017). *Behind the Velvet Ropes of Facebook's Private Groups*, The New York Times. https://www.nytimes.com/2017/07/16/business/behind-the-velvet-ropes-of-facebooks-private-groups.html

Roose, K. (June 8, 2019). *The Making of a YouTube Radical*, The New York Times. https://www.nytimes.com/interactive/2019/06/08/technology/youtube-radical.html

Rowley, J., and Farrow, J. (2000). *Organizing knowledge: an introduction to managing access to information* (3rd Ed.), Aldershot: Gower.

Rubinstein, Z. (2021). Taxing Big Data: A Proposal to Benefit Society for the Use of Private Information. *Fordham Intellectual Property, Media and Entertainment Law Journal, 31*(4), pp. 1241–1244.

Santario, A. (May 6, 2018). *What the GDPR, Europe's Tough New Data Law, Means for You*, The New York Times. https://www.nytimes.com/2018/05/06/technology/gdpr-european-privacy-law.html

Samuelson, P. A. (1948). Consumption Theory in Terms of Revealed Preference. *Economica, New Series, 15*(60), pp. 243–253.

Schneider, V. (2020). Locked Out by Big Data: How Big Data, Algorithms and Machine Learning May Undermine Housing Justice. *Columbia Human Rights Law Review, 52*(1), pp. 251–305.

Schneier, B. (2015). *Data and Goliath: The Hidden Battles to Collect Your Data and Control Your World*, New York: W.W. Norton & Company.

Sebastão, D., and Borges, S. (2021). Should we stay or should we go: EU input legitimacy under threat? Social media and Brexit. *Transforming Government, People, Process and Policy, 15*(3), pp. 335–346.

Seaver, N. (2019). Captivating algorithms: Recommender systems as traps. *Journal of Material Culture, 24*(4), pp. 421–436.

Solove, D. J. (2006). A Taxonomy of Privacy. *University of Pennsylvania Law Review, 154*, pp. 477–560.

Solove, D. J. (2008). *Understanding Privacy*, Harvard: University Press.

Stachl, C., Au, Q., Schoedel, R., Gosling, S. D., Harari, G. M., Buschek, D., Völkel, S. T., Schuwerk, T., Oldemeier, M., Ullmann, T., Hussmann, H., Bischl, B., and Bühner, M. (2020). Predicting personality from patterns of behavior collected with smartphones. *Proceedings of the National Academy of Sciences, 117*(30), pp. 17680–17687, doi: 10.1073/pnas.1920484117.

Stalder, F. (2002). Privacy is not the Antidote to Surveillance. *Surveillance and Society, 1*(1), pp. 120–124.

Stephens-Davidowitz, S. (2017). *Everybody Lies*, New York: Dey Street Books.

Stöcker, C. (2020). How Facebook and Google Accidentally Created a Perfect Ecosystem for Targeted Disinformation. In C. Grimme, M. Preuss, F. W. Takes, and A. Waldherr (Eds.), *Proceedings of MISDOOM 2019: Disinformation in Open Online Media*, Berlin: Springer, pp. 129–149.

Stolton, S. (2021). *German legal dispute over Facebook data use sent to European Court of Justice*. Euractiv, https://www.euractiv.com/section/data-protection/news/german-legal-dispute-over-facebook-data-use-sent-to-european-court-of-justice/.

Susarla, A. (January 28, 2020). *Hate cancel culture? Blame algorithms*, The Conversation. https://theconversation.com/hate-cancel-culture-blame-algorithms-129402

Susskind, L., and McMahon, G. (1985). The Theory and Practice of Negotiated Rulemaking. *Yale Journal on Regulation, 3*(1), pp.133–165.

Temkin, D. (March 3, 2021). Charting a course towards a more privacy-first web, Google Ads & Commerce Blog.

Termeer, C. J. A. M., and Kessener, B. (2007). Revitalizing Stagnated Policy Processes: Using the Configuration Approach for Research and Interventions. *The Journal of Applied Behavioral Science, 43*(2), pp. 256–272.

Termeer, C. J. A. M., Dewulf, A., Breeman, G., and Stiller, S. J. (2015). Governance Capabilities for Dealing Wisely With Wicked Problems. *Administration & Society, 47*(6), pp. 680–710.

Thomas, R. (2019). *Getting Specific About Algorithmic Bias*, https://www.youtube.com/watch?v=S-6YGPrmtYc.

Thompson, S. A. (April 30, 2019). *These Ads Think They Know You*, The New York Times.https://www.nytimes.com/interactive/2019/04/30/opinion/privacy-targeted-advertising.html

Tufekci, Z. (April 21, 2019). *Think You're Discreet Online? Think Again*, The New York Times.https://www.nytimes.com/2019/04/21/opinion/computational-inference.html

Umoja, N. S. (2018). *Algorithms of Oppression: How Search Engines Reinforce Racism*, New York: University Press.

van Vliet, M., and Dubbink, W. (2018). Evaluating Governance: State, Market and Participation Compared. In J. Kooiman, M van Vliet and S. Jentoft (Eds.), *Creative Governance*, London: Routledge, doi: org/10.4324/9780429463761.

Wachter, S. and Mittelstadt, B. (2019). A Right to Reasonable Inferences: Re-Thinking Data Protection Law in the Age of Big Data and AI. *Columbia Business Law Review, 2019*(2), pp. 494–620, doi: 10.7916/cblr.v2019i2.3424.

Wadhwa, T. (2020). *Economic Impact and Feasibility of Data Dividends*, Washington DC: Data Catalyst.

Watson, M. (2019). *YouTube is Facilitating the Sexual Exploitation of Children, and it's Being Monetized*, https://www.youtube.com/watch?v=O13G5A5w5Po.

Westin A. F. (1967). *Privacy and freedom*, New York: Atheneum.

Williams, B. A., Brooks, C. F., and Shmargad, Y. (2018). How Algorithms Discriminate Based on Data They Lack: Challenges, Solutions, and Policy Implications. *Journal of Information Policy, 8*, pp. 78–115.

Wisniewski, P. J., Knijnenburg, B. P., and Lipford, H. R. (2017). Making privacy personal: Profiling social network users to inform privacy education and nudging. *International Journal of Human-Computer Studies, 98*, pp. 95–108.

Yeh, C-L. (2018). Pursuing consumer empowerment in the age of big data: A comprehensive regulatory framework for data brokers. *Telecommunications Policy*, 42(4), pp. 282–292.

Yeung, K. (2017). 'Hypernudge': Big Data as a mode of regulation by design. *Information, Communication & Society*, 20(1), pp. 118–136, doi: 10.1080/1369118X.2016.1186713.

Youyou, W., Kosinski, M., and Stillwell, D. (2015). Computers judge personalities better than humans. *Proceedings of the National Academy of Sciences*, 112(4), pp. 1036–1040.

Zarouali, B., Dobber, T., De Pauw, G., and de Vreese, C. (2020). Using a Personality-Profiling Algorithm to Investigate Political Microtargeting: Assessing the Persuasion Effects of Personality-Tailored Ads on Social Media, *Communication Research*, doi: 0093650220961965.

Zeleny, M. (1987). Management Support Systems: Towards Integrated Knowledge Management. *Human Systems Management*, 7(1), pp. 59–70.

Zuboff, S. (2015). Big Other: Surveillance Capitalism and the Prospects of an Information Civilization. *Journal of Information Technology*, 30(1), pp. 75–89.

Zuboff, S. (March 5, 2016). *The Secrets of Surveillance Capitalism*, Frankfurter Allgemeine Zeitung. https://www.faz.net/aktuell/feuilleton/debatten/the-digital-debate/shoshana-zuboff-secrets-of-surveillance-capitalism-14103616.html

Zollo, F., and Quattrociocchi, W. (2018). Misinformation spreading on Facebook. In S. Lehmann and Y-Y., Ahn (Eds), *Complex Spreading Phenomena in Social Systems*. Berlin: Springer, pp. 177–196.

Zuiderveen Borgesius, F. J., Möller, J., Kruikemeier, S., Ó Fathaigh, R., Irion, K., Dobber, T., Bodo, B., and de Vreese, C. (2018). Online Political Microtargeting: Promises and Threats for Democracy, *Utrecht Law Review*, 14(1), pp. 1–96.

Printed and bound by CPI Group (UK) Ltd, Croydon, CR0 4YY

13/04/2025

14656542-0001